MAKE THEM BEHAVE SUSTAINABLY

D1702265

ADRIANA OLAYA RODRIGUEZ

ISBN: 978-1984221070
Front cover image by Adriana Olaya Rodriguez.
Book design by Adriana Olaya Rodriguez.
Editing by HappyMarli.
All illustrations and photographs by Adriana Olaya Rodriguez unless otherwise credited.

Printed and distributed by CreateSpace and Amazon.com
First printing, 2018.

www.makethembehave.com

ABOUT THE AUTHOR

Adriana Olaya Rodriguez is a passionate design thinker. She graduated from the Pontificia Universidad Javeriana in Colombia with a BA in Industrial Design, followed by an MSc in Eco-Design from the Politecnico di Torino in Italy. Along with her academic background in systemic and sustainable design, Adriana has a proven track record in business storytelling and design research.

Even at her young age and in the early stages of her career, Adriana has provided strategic guidance and project delivery management on a broad range of projects for different types of organizations — from the retail sector, private companies, service industries up to the public and governmental sectors — including the European Commission, UNICEF, 3M, UNDP, and the Chamber of Commerce of Bogotá, among others.

She is a dedicated vegetarian, a sustainable lifestyle activist, an animal lover and a high-quality-service addict. Even as a child, Adriana explored her great curiosity concerning environmental aspects, which later (with her academic and professional experience) turned into a deep interest in systemic design and circular economy to achieve sustainable development.

In 2015, Adriana was selected to be the Sustainability Reporter of the Nudge Sustainable Hub to write reports about sustainable projects in Colombia and around the world. This was followed in 2017 by a fellowship in the program 'International Climate Protection Fellowship for young climate experts from developing countries' through the Alexander von Humboldt Foundation to conduct research on her two favorite topics: design and sustainable consumption.

ACKNOWLEDGMENTS

I would like to thank the Alexander von Humboldt Foundation, which funded my research stay in Germany, as well as bauchplan).(for their advice and support. I would also like to thank all the researchers, writers and organizations mentioned in this book that have been such a great source of inspiration for my work.
To all those in Colombia, Germany, Italy, Belgium and the USA who have kindly assisted this book in various ways—thank you!
Above all, I would like to thank my family for their immeasurable support and for making me the person I am, someone who cares and who is committed to the planet, society and the environment. Thank you for being my inspiration, motivation, and the motor of my life.

FOREWORD by bauchplan).(

Adriana Olaya is a sustainable design thinker and doer. In this work, she presents a compelling and practical framework for how designers can use a holistic approach to address the severe and interrelated worldwide problems of unsustainable consumption and climate change. Adriana offers readers, students, business leaders, designers, and policy makers the tools, strategies, and practical pathways they need to successfully drive consumers towards sustainable consumption. Far more than a rhetorical exercise, this book is designed to inform, inspire, and affect action.

We, as a collective of urban planners and landscape architects, have engaged with the issue of bringing urban food production back into the everyday lives of metropolitan citizens for a long time. Herein, sustainable interaction between people and public spaces has played a crucial role. In 2009, bauchplan).(, as an interdisciplinary team, won a competition - wherein the goal was to create an urban food strategy – with our project Agropolis. This marked the beginning of a transnational movement to strengthen the awareness of soil as a resource, as well as the potential of green urban spaces and landscapes.

The overarching aim was to counteract urbanites' alienation towards their day-to-day consumption of food and to highlight the possibility of direct access to this valuable resource. Above all, however, it allowed the realization of sustainable behavior patterns that can be experienced through food and nutrition on a daily basis.

Over the years, we turned the fundamental aspects of this ambitious project into reality and actively participated in an integrative city development process, which resulted in our innovative outdoor supermarket, The Freiluftsupermarkt. The project sought not only to increase the awareness of soil as a resource, but also to promote a sustainable integration of people in their neighborhood. We became aware of our responsibility to create structures that allow social and ecological values to be balanced in equally sustainable measures in the spatial and conceptual realization.

Initiated in Munich and Vienna, the project brought together people from all over the world, from different age groups and nationalities, as well as from varying socio-economic groups in one place with the purpose of sowing, weeding, harvesting and celebrating.

It was in the early stages of the project that Adriana Olaya joined us to not only conduct field research in the Freiluftsupermarkt, but also to actively participate in it. At that point, her interest in sustainable development driven by smart design solutions was already substantial. The project reaffirmed Adriana's perception that even just a single consumer could contribute to the sustainable management of resources through a conscious lifestyle, and that such mentality can also have an effect on other areas of life.

Since the beginning, our work has been to create spaces of possibility, places in which disparate needs are given space, next to and with each other. In our view, they should also possess so much potential for realization that autonomous adoption by their owners should be possible without being restricted by a narrow set of requirements.

In recognition of this, the National German Sustainability Award was granted to our project wagnisART last year, after having already won several other prizes. It is a recognition concerning the necessity of working on a concept for open land use together with those that would be using it. The creation and the needs of the community were combined with a great degree of sensitivity.

As planners, our task consists not only of observing and adopting specific usage patterns, but also of developing a model for sustainable interaction with one's social and ecological environment.

Thus, a sustainable way of life is not a question of economic standards, but should instead be at everyone's disposal. Here, the role of the designer is crucial both in the context of landscape and design, because they are able to influence, push and advance the sustainable development agenda.

This is why Adriana's work is truly profound for us, our profession, as well as all those interested in sustainability. To host a Humboldtian at our office has been a great honor, to acknowledge not only how the topic of her research constitutes such an essential part of our work, but also the opportunity to measure our ideals in discussions and contributions on an international scale. Spending time and sharing knowledge with Adriana was a great pleasure, and we are extremely proud of her having reached an important milestone in her research.

We hope that for many of its readers, this book will demonstrate how important it is to put humans as the consumers of design at the core of any sustainability consideration, an experience that they can then use as a tool towards more sustainable everyday realities.

CONT

11 BASICS

Let's make a real difference for the planet, for the economy, and for the people

ENTS

INTRODUCTION

The enormous rise of globalization and capitalism has made it possible to produce more, cheaper and faster products; consequently, the life cycle of goods (products and services), from production, through consumption, to eventual disposal, is accelerated and shortened. The global economy is exceeding the sustainable carrying capacity of the planet, and this has been going on for some time. According to a report of the United Nations Environment Programme (UNEP)[94], global material extraction (non-metallic minerals, metal ores, fossil fuels and biomass) has increased substantially over the years. In 1970, the global amount of materials extracted was around 20 billion tons. In that same year, the global population was around 3.68 billion[69]. By 2013, the population had reached 7.21 billion and the materials extracted had increased to almost 85 billion tons. In other words, during the same period of time, the global population almost doubled (1.9x), but the amount of materials extracted more than quadrupled (4.2x).

This trend is being driven by the escalation and expansion of the western consumer lifestyle, which is highly resource- and energy-intensive, and cannot be sustained due to the limited resources available to mankind. Calculations show that the planet has 1.9 hectares of biologically productive land per person available to supply resources and absorb wastes. However, the average person on earth already uses 2.3 hectares. These 'ecological footprints' range from the 9.7 hectares claimed by the average American to the 0.47 hectares used by the average Mozambican [104].

Americans and Western Europeans have primarily contributed to this unsustainable over-consumption rate for decades, but now, developing countries are catching up rapidly and contributing to the detriment of the environment and to climate change with their consumption patterns. By the year 2000, nearly half of global consumers resided in developing countries, including China and India—markets with the most potential for expansion, according to the Worldwatch Institute [105]. Today, these figures continue to rise and will represent major consumption growth both in developed and developing countries.

To change these increasing, contemporary and unsustainable consumer societies, we must first understand how they work. After gaining these insights, we can develop new structures that facilitate practices of sustainable consumption. Our lifestyle decisions, especially concerning our consumption, are made within social, economic and political constraints. Those structures determine how easy or difficult, necessary or impossible it is to make a lifestyle decision. The challenge of achieving sustainable production and consumption strongly influences the design of more sustainable products, services, processes, strategies and consumption patterns (later in the book referred to as sustainable interventions) by policy makers, businesses and consumers alike.

In the industry, designers shape the development of products and services that directly impact society and the environment. According to the Environmental Change Institute [21], over 80% of the product-related environmental impact is determined during the product design phase. Along these lines, designers need to take moral responsibility for the outcomes of human interaction with products and services. Hence, the application of sustainable design strategies to promote sustainable consumption and lifestyles reduces not only the life cycle impact, but also the consumer ecological footprint. Therefore, the main challenge is to design the use phase of products and services in a way that makes consumers link available information, their behavior and the environmental and social impact.

The key role of designers linking manufacturing processes and consumers is not limited to the design of products and services; they must also seek alternative solutions to the wasteful lifestyles of contemporary society. Their role is to influence positive change through the creation of more responsible and sustainable interventions and goods.

This book is intended to offer readers an integral perspective about strategies to change consumer behavior and promote sustainable consumption. It combines theories, concepts and methodologies from a variety of disciplines to facilitate the conception and design process of sustainable products, services, processes, strategies and consumption patterns, from start to finish. Taking into consideration the variety of consumer types and the process that the human brain undertakes to perform any behavior, from the internal and external factors that influence it, to the motivation, ability and prompts necessary to perform it, this book explains sustainable design and consumer behavior change strategies and instruments. Using the roadmap tool, it suggests a path for readers to follow that will ease both their understanding and the practical process.

With this book, I hope to inspire constant improvement to make a real difference for the environment, the people, the economy and the planet. I invite you to always keep in mind that we are all in this together. We need a global commitment to sustainability if we want to live in a responsible, safe and prosperous world, and most importantly, if we want to give this to our children and future generations. Designers, entrepreneurs, business leaders, creatives, marketers, policymakers and anyone else who has the power to influence or change the living conditions of one person, or an entire society, must act ethically, thinking about the well-being of the people and the environment. We must stop and reflect: What am I doing to make this world a better place? What is the impact of my actions? How can I ensure better living conditions for the people and the environment I influence with my work and behavior? In that moment, every one of us has the power to make a positive change.

There is no doubt that for me, writing this book was a labor of altruism, love, and commitment for a sustainable future.
For you, I hope reading it will be as well.

I invite you to always keep in mind that we are all in this together. We need a global commitment to sustainability if we want to live in a responsible, safe and prosperous world.

BASICS
ROADMAP
CASES

MAKE THEM BEHAVE SUSTAINABLY

This book is divided into three main sections. **BASICS** presents the fundamental concepts based on a literature review concerning consumer behavior, human behavior and habits. Furthermore, (design) strategies and instruments are promoted for more sustainable consumption. Given this knowledge, the subsequent section, **ROADMAP**, develops a tool to assist the design process in order to produce sustainable and innovative solutions to change consumer behavior. The **CASES** section highlights different companies, projects and governmental strategies that are forerunners in terms of sustainable production and consumption strategies.

DEFINITIONS, VOCABULARY & TERMS

Designers: In this book, I refer to designers in a broad sense as anyone that is in charge of designing a product, process, marketing campaign, intervention or event, among others. The term includes all those who change the environment with the inspiration of human creativity, especially industrial designers or service designers, but also anyone who is implicit in the conception and realization of human needs, desires and satisfiers (the means by which people satisfy fundamental human needs).

Sustainable consumption: The definition proposed by the 1994 Oslo Symposium on Sustainable Consumption defines this as "the use of services and related products which respond to basic needs and bring a better quality of life while minimizing the use of natural resources and toxic materials, as well as emissions of waste and pollutants, over the life cycle of the service or product so as not to jeopardize the needs of future generations."

Sustainable development: Sustainable development is development that meets the needs of the present without compromising the ability of future generations to meet their own needs. It aims at a positive environmental, social and economic balance.

Service design: An emerging design field focused on the creation of well-planned experiences using a combination of intangible and tangible mediums that also determine the compound impacts of it, routing development, and how future decisions are made. Service design as a practice generally results in the design of systems and processes aimed at providing a holistic service to the user. This cross-disciplinary practice combines numerous skills in design, management and process engineering. The work of the designer is highly focused on the touch points where the user interacts with the design. It is mostly through these points that a designer can influence the outcome of the service and the behavior of the user.

Eco-design: The design of a product or service that applies environmental criteria aimed at the prevention of waste and emissions, as well as the minimization of their environmental impact, throughout the life cycle of the product.

Sustainable behavior: Using a product or service in a way that has less of a negative and harmful impact on the environment and reduces the consumer ecological footprint, in comparison to conventional ways of using similar products or services.

Design for Behavior Change (DfBC): is a design field that acknowledges designers' responsibility and attempts to facilitate a shift in the everyday choices of the population to create a positive change and to close the so-called 'value-action gap' between people's attitudes, which are often pro-environmental, and their everyday behavior. Behavioral Design is being applied to solve challenges related to consumer behavior, organizational behavior and public behavior.

Sustainable interventions: In this book, I refer to this term as sustainable products, services, processes, strategies and consumption patterns.

Intention-behavior gap: This gap refers to the difference between the intention and the actual result of the behavior. For example, although some people may develop the intention to change their behavior towards sustainability, they might not take any action for various reasons.

ICONOGRAPHY

To help you understand and remember the useful information in this book, the most relevant concepts in the text are matched with graphics and figures. To facilitate the identification and comprehension of the meaning of the elements, the following icons are used in this book:

Consumer

Business/ industry

Government

Service/ Product

Unsustainable Service/ Product

Sustainable Service/ Product

Facilitator strategies

Design intervention

Evaluation

Enthusiastic consumer

Irresponsible consumer

Undecided consumer

Worried consumer

Consumer behavior

Sustainable consumer behavior

Prompt

Motivation

Ability

BASICS

fundamental concepts based on literature review

SUSTAINABLE CONSUMPTION & THE ROLE OF DESIGNERS

BASICS

Each year, 1.3 billion tons of food, equivalent to one-third of all food produced – worth around $1 trillion – ends up as waste, partly in the bins of consumers and retailers. According to the UN [91], modern households consume 29% of global energy, which represents 21% of total CO_2 emissions. Disturbing facts like those are the reality, not only of the food and energy sector, but of almost every resource we consume: water, soil, technology, clothing, household products, transportation, meat, etc. Now imagine the increase in these figures in the future. Globally, more people are expected to join the middle class over the next two decades. This is certainly good for individual prosperity and the global eradication of poverty, but at the same time, it will increase the demand for the planet's already constrained natural resources.

Until now, the main sources of ecological impact have been production processes and the material selection of products and services. However, today's social reality related to climate change is reshaping this condition. Preventive measures for a sustainable future also consider the configuration of products and services with respect to how they are designed to be consumed. In order to successfully change, the challenge lies in the shift of the concept and trajectory of how societies have been created and shaped.

This shift implies a change in the expectations of how the future of living, working and consuming should look. It also requires a massive redesign of products and services, industrial practices, policies and consumer lifestyles to offer people the means to express their chosen identity in a sustainable way.

According to the Brundtland Commission, sustainability encounters a set of guiding principles and key objectives, particularly the acceptance of limits and the priority for satisfying human needs without compromising the ability of future generations to meet their own needs [102].
For this reason, sustainable development requires that policy makers, industry leaders and the mainstream population adopt and promote lifestyles based on the limitations of ecological resources.

Therefore, both in industrial and governmental institutions, designers play a crucial role in ensuring more sustainable consumer habits and lifestyles. As mentioned before, the highest percentage of the product-related environmental impact is generated by the product design phase.

More precisely, designers are able to bridge the intention-behavior gap, which defines the difference between the intention of consumers' environmental values and the actual result of their behavior in everyday actions [79].

To address this situation, actions to reduce greenhouse emissions and the environmental impact of products and services should engage the whole life cycle. For many goods, the use phase contributes the most to the total environmental impact, but designers are now being challenged to reduce the impact by applying strategies to design sustainable consumer behavior [45].

DESIGN
RESPONSIBILITY?
80%
OF THE ENVIRONMENTAL
IMPACT
IS DETERMINED IN THE
DESIGN PHASE

Environmentally significant behavior and the threat of the intention-behavior gap

The first step in changing unsustainable lifestyles and decision-making, for both consumers and producers, is to understand the real impact of their behavior on the environment. Stern [74] defines this as environmentally significant behavior based on two different perspectives. The first recognizes environmentally significant behavior as having a positive or negative impact on the natural environment, considering the real and factual impact of it. The second perspective takes the consumer perspective, namely the intent to act in an environmentally significant way, most often with the aim of having a positive impact. That means this second perspective relates to consumers' thoughts about the positive or negative impacts of their behavior without having sufficient, correct or concrete information about it.

Stern sees these two perspectives as a contradiction that leads to a gap between what people think is environmentally significant and the total impact that can be attributed to the behavior over the entire life cycle.

For example, many Germans have increased their organic product consumption, as they want to minimize their contribution to the impact of chemical pesticides and fertilizers on the environment. However, in many cases, the long-distance transport, processing, large amount of plastic packaging and the distribution of this organic food produced in distant countries will have a higher impact on the environment than if no organic products were involved. Thus, consumer behavior inevitably becomes detrimental to the environment.

Imported organic vs. Local conventional.

A study performed in 2011 on the significance of transport for the carbon footprint of imported organic plant products found that organic soybeans from China imported to Denmark have a higher carbon footprint than local conventional production of the same product [87]. With a focus on the environmental effects of the farming systems, the results show that the organic soybeans produced in the case study area in China have a lower environmental impact than conventional production with regard to greenhouse gas emissions, nutrient enrichment and use of non-renewable energy. Half of the carbon footprint from organic soybeans from China was related to transport. This finding is in agreement with British studies, which showed that transport accounted for approximately 40-70% of the carbon footprint of imported plant products transported by ship and/or truck.

However, the carbon footprint of every product varies according to the production system, the resources activated and the mode of transportation.

Consumers thinking about their impact on the environment | **Real impact** on the environment

The gap discussed earlier between the actual environmental impact of a behavior and what people think it entails can be due to insufficient knowledge about the general environmental impact of consumption, as well as their own consumption habits, in particular.

Another misstep with respect to environmentally significant behavior is to focus perception on the few areas in which the behavior is more sustainable, ignoring other areas in which the behavior is less sustainable. For example, a person might feel quite sustainable in their behavior by separating their trash for recycling and taking public transport to work. However, at the same time, that person might ignore the impact caused by their frequent use of air travel[75].

Similarly, some industries have the good intention of replacing less environmentally friendly materials without accounting for the entire life cycle. In some cases, although the new materials have better properties in terms of recyclability and reusability, the extraction of the raw material might be more harmful to the surrounding ecosystems and/or the transformation requires significant amounts of energy and resources. Consequently, the companies' introspection in terms of positive environmental impact increases, but their actual impact is more negative than before.
It is therefore necessary to establish a better and deeper understanding of the impact to generate awareness of the environmental significance of the behavior.

Aluminum vs. Glass

Bottled and canned drinks are a big business worldwide. The use of aluminum as a substitute for glass bottles has been growing in the market in recent years as a more sustainable substitute for the packaging of beverages. For these two materials, the extraction and manufacturing processes have the largest environmental impact.

On the one hand, glass is made from non-renewable resources: sand, silica and limestone. This material requires energy to heat them to 1200°C in a furnace during manufacture. In addition, despite the recyclability properties of glass, its heavy weight increases the CO_2 emissions due to the fuel needed for transportation.
On the other hand, aluminum is made from bauxite, mined from open-pit or dredging mines, which have several damaging environmental impacts. Aluminum processing is water- and energy-intensive and produces a variety of pollutants. Primary aluminum production accounts for more than 90% of the total environmental footprint of making aluminum cans. Aluminum can be recycled repeatedly without limit. This recycling factor and its lightweight nature is what incentivizes so many industries to use aluminum. Despite its recycling potential, Annie Leonard, the founder of the Story of Stuff [47], notes that only 45% of cans are currently being recycled.

The beverage industry, in order to increase environmentally significant behavior, must select the material by considering that if aluminum cans are made from 100% recycled aluminum, it's the best choice for the packaging of drinks. If the material is not recycled, glass bottles have a lower carbon footprint, especially if the bottles are refilled and the distribution distance is short.

Sustainable lifestyle

To achieve a significant collective change in how societies are shaped, we must reconsider many aspects of our personal lifestyle and examine our daily consumption habits. Durning [19] considers the questions of how much is enough and what level of consumption the planet can support. In 2017, the Earth Overshoot Day fell on August 2 [20]. This day marks the date when humanity has exhausted nature's budget for the year. It means that we used more from nature than our planet can renew in the whole year, due to overfishing, overharvesting forests, and emitting more carbon dioxide into the atmosphere than forests can sequester. In other words, in 2017, we lived in debt to the planet and our natural resources in just over half a year, exhausting and deteriorating the planet without the possibility of recovering the only source of resources we have to survive – Earth.

TIME WE LIVED
IN DEBT
WITH NATURE
DURING 2017

August 2.
Earth Overshoot Day.
We **exhausted** nature's budget
of the year

With psychological studies, Durning argues that, according to data, <u>consumption is not a main determinant of happiness. Instead, it is prominently related to family life and work satisfaction, leisure and friendship.</u>
In his opinion, technological change will need to be complemented with curbing our material wants. It is evident that today's western consumer lifestyle is opposed to long-term social and ecological sustainability [95].

Consumption is not a main determinant of happiness.
Instead, it is prominently related with family life and work satisfaction, leisure and friendship.

Sustainable consumption

Consumption involves the selection, purchase, use, maintenance, repair, disposal and recycling of any product or service [44]. Although consumption tends to be a major part of the life cycle by definition, it still does not receive appropriate attention with respect to sustainability. The focus is still largely on the improvement of production, but not the consumption patterns. For instance, the energy sector is presently developing new technologies to generate cleaner and more efficient energy in order to produce more and satisfy the high market demand with lower CO_2 emissions. However, the problem should not be addressed by producing more efficiently and therefore being able to consume more, but rather by decreasing overall consumption. In other words, emissions should be decreased not only through the use of renewable technologies, but also by the amount being consumed.

According to this principle, the SustainAbility team published its findings about the market implications of sustainable lifestyle research in a report with the title: *Who Needs It?* [76]. The message was that people should not just buy greener, but buy less, suggesting that consumption should be driven by needs over wants. Certain goods and services are simply unnecessary, while others are consumed in excess. There is also a trend of unsustainable shopping on a global scale. One of the challenges is to meet non-material needs through non-material means; by buying less and deriving satisfaction elsewhere, this can be achieved.

Sustainable consumption and production (SCP) is "the use of services and related products, which respond to basic needs and brings a better quality of life while minimizing the use of natural resources and toxic materials, as well as the emissions of waste and pollutants, over the life cycle of the service or product so as not to jeopardize the needs of further generations".

- The Oslo Symposium in 1994

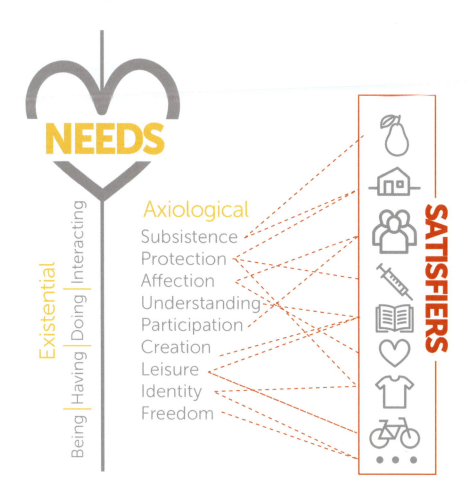

NEEDS

Existential

Being | Having | Doing | Interacting

Axiological
Subsistence
Protection
Affection
Understanding
Participation
Creation
Leisure
Identity
Freedom

SATISFIERS

Max-Neef [49] classifies fundamental human needs into two categories: existential and axiological. The existential needs are Being, Having, Doing and Interacting. The needs of Subsistence, Protection, Affection, Understanding, Participation, Creation, Leisure, Identity and Freedom are classified as axiological. The means by which humans satisfy these needs are the satisfiers.

According to this categorization, food and shelter must be considered satisfiers of the fundamental need for Subsistence, not as basic needs. In the same way, any kind of education and the education system, in general, are satisfiers of the Understanding need.

There is no one-to-one correspondence between needs and satisfiers. A need may require various satisfiers to be met, or conversely, a satisfier may satisfy different needs. These relations may vary depending on time, place and circumstances.

The choice of satisfiers is a main aspect that defines a culture. Each economic, social and political system adopts different systems and methods for the satisfaction of the same fundamental human needs through the generation (or non-generation) of different types of satisfiers. No matter which society a person belongs to, the fundamental human needs are always the same. What changes is the choice of the quantity and quality of satisfiers. Therefore, what is culturally determined are the satisfiers, rather than the needs. Cultural change is, among other things, the consequence of discontinuing or changing traditional satisfiers.

Obviously, many needs are best satisfied by non-commercial services, such as family care or being among friends, rather than by products. However, in the capitalist world in which we live, sustainable design, production and consumption should be understood as choosing true satisfiers, rather than about neglecting needs.

For this reason, designers play a key role in defining and providing satisfiers that fulfill both the needs of the market and the goals for sustainable development, which largely depends on awareness of the importance of sustainable consumption.

PEOPLE SHOULD NOT JUST BUY GREENER BUT LESS

The role of designers in creating a sustainable future

In 2016 each of the 195 member countries of the United Nations Framework Convention on Climate Change (UNFCCC) signed the Paris Agreement. The agreement deals with greenhouse gas emission mitigation and adaptation. It establishes the goal of strengthening the global response to the threat of climate change. In this century, the global temperature rise should be kept well below 2 degrees Celsius above pre-industrial levels.
In order to meet this goal, each country must determine, plan and regularly report its own contribution to mitigating global warming.

This means that, aside from other measures, sustainable consumption and the production of tomorrow to meet the 2030 Sustainable Development Goals (SDGs) requires a massive redesign of consumer goods and industrial practices of services and infrastructures in order to reach the goal.

According to the 2030 SDGs, the so-called 'Responsible consumption and production' goal intends to promote resource and energy efficiency, sustainable infrastructure, and provide access to basic services, green and decent jobs and a better quality of life for all [92].

"Sustainable consumption and production aims at 'doing more and better with less,' increasing net welfare gains from economic activities by reducing resource use, degradation and pollution along the whole life cycle, while increasing quality of life. It involves different stakeholders, including businesses, consumers, policy makers, researchers, scientists, retailers, media, and development cooperation agencies, among others.
It also requires a systemic approach and cooperation among actors operating in the supply chain, from producer to final consumer. It involves engaging consumers through awareness-raising and education on sustainable consumption and lifestyles, providing consumers with adequate information through standards and labels and engaging in sustainable public procurement, among others" (United Nations, 2018).

Previous studies [50, 88] have reviewed the activities of designers, demonstrating their key role in linking the manufacturing process and consumers. Both industrial and service designers play a significant role in seeking alternative solutions to the wasteful lifestyle of contemporary society, and in influencing positive change through the creation of more responsible and sustainable goods.

We (Countries) commit to making fundamental changes in the way that our societies produce and consume goods and services. Governments, international organizations, the business sector and other non-state actors and individuals must contribute to changing unsustainable consumption and production patterns, including through the mobilization, from all sources, of financial and technical assistance to strengthen developing countries' scientific, technological and innovative capacities to move towards more sustainable patterns of consumption and production. We encourage the implementation of the 10-Year Framework of Programmes on Sustainable Consumption and Production. All countries take action, with developed countries taking the lead, taking into account the development and capabilities of developing countries.

- Goal n.12 Paragraph 28 of the 2030 Agenda for Sustainable Development

With those facts in mind, experts have stressed that design education should be redirected to the development of an ethical designer [25, 24], one who could rethink and radically design interventions that redirect environmental problems. This means that designers need to take ethical and moral responsibility for their own actions, due to the consequences of human interactions with artifacts, goods and services.

If you are creating an intervention that will be liberally distributed, used, and will probably end as waste around the country or across the world, then it is crucial to ask yourself ethical questions like why, when, how, and what happens next. Unfortunately, sustainability plays a minor role in design education and practice thus far, because design is still not recognized as a relevant factor in the sustainability discourse.

However, design as a tool for consumer behavior change, with sustainability as its purpose, has recently gained considerable interest. This slow process of change is due to the essential action of choosing the right design intervention and strategy for each particular combination of behaviors and individuals.
Conventional sustainable design approaches mostly participate in reducing environmental impact by implementing product-focused strategies. These strategies mostly concentrate on technological and material properties, such as the use of recycled or recyclable materials during manufacturing, increasing resource efficiency, effectiveness, and achieving product longevity.

Nevertheless, the way people use a product contributes immensely to the negative impact on the environment as never seen before. For instance, researchers found that the majority of the impact of products can be attributed to user behavior [51,103]. Thus, promoting sustainable consumption practices is crucial for sustainability, going hand in hand with designing sustainable products and services.
These sustainable consumption practices and pro-environmental behaviors can be derived from a huge range of actions, such as minimizing resources and energy consumption, recycling, using sustainable modes of transportation, being a member of an environmental institution, etc.

It is indeed true that designers have both the opportunity and the relevant skills to develop such products to enhance positive behavior change, especially when playing an active role in the intervention development process, particularly in the early stages. A systemic way to scale up and mainstream sustainable consumption is to design and provide interventions that promote these three principles: (a) the sharing of goods and services; (b) the downsizing of goods and services by consuming less; and (c) the shifting towards more resource-efficient products and services (sustainable production).

In the literature about Design for Behavior Change (DfBC), Design for the Environment (DfE) and Design for Sustainability (DfS), many strategies and instruments can be found to help designers promote more sustainable consumer behavior. Some of these instruments will be explained in the following chapters.

Designers need to take ethical and moral responsibility for their own actions, due to the consequences of human interactions with artifacts, goods and services.

ACTORS INVOLVED IN THE CHANGE

BASICS

In society, there are always three main groups linked with the products, services and infrastructures that people use: people, business and government. They represent the Triangle of Change. According to the Sustainable Consumption Roundtable report *I will if you will* [79], these three groups fundamentally have the clout to embed more sustainable consumption habits. Government and business have the major responsibility to focus their strategies, policies and innovations towards mainstream consumers to achieve sustainable development. The responsibility to change the market should not exclusively lie on the already more sustainable consumers.

By making sustainable products the norm, the government and industries can enable consumers to make sustainable choices. In this way, people who are ready and willing to change their behavior in favor of climate protection and sustainable consumption will have support from the newly introduced policies to achieve this goal. Consequently, the circle of action will be enlarged. People seeing others acting around them and feeling that their efforts are worthwhile will boost their motivation to continue acting sustainably.

A combination of incentives, community initiatives and local feedback will reassure people that they are part of a collective movement that is making a real difference, rather than thinking they are a minority making efforts without any impact.

These three groups fundamentally have the clout to embed more sustainable consumption habits.

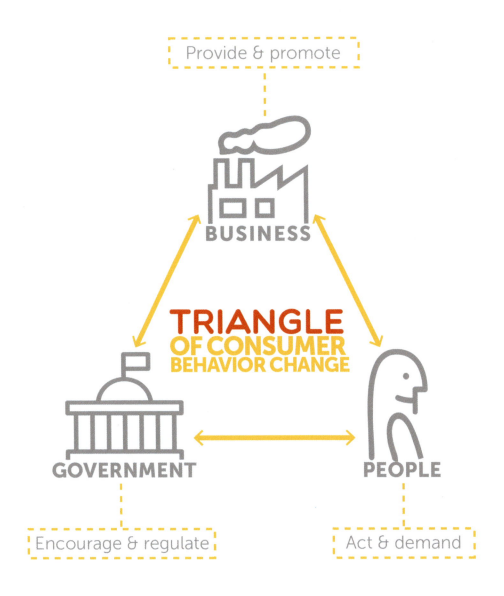

Provide & promote

BUSINESS

TRIANGLE
OF CONSUMER
BEHAVIOR CHANGE

GOVERNMENT

PEOPLE

Encourage & regulate

Act & demand

Government

New interventions and technologies require modifications in the market and a change in business practices.
Political leadership is crucial to encourage more sustainable consumption habits. The purpose of public policy on sustainable consumption should be to encourage, enable, and engage governments, municipalities, the business sector and civil society to make it easier for consumers to act sustainably and move progressively towards sustainable development.

With the creation and application of a Sustainable Consumption Action Framework (when the master framework changes from theory to action using principles, procedures and structure), governments change consumption habits and promote sustainable ones through supportive policies and practices. The aim is to shift values in society and create profitable opportunities for all companies to deliver more sustainable services and products.

In other words, a Sustainable Consumption Action Framework (SCAF) is a guide for policy makers that enables behavior change. A successful SCAF consists of five elements, according to the Sustainable Consumption Roundtable report [79]:

1. **Use the mandate for action.** A governmental mandate can contribute significantly to help people change their behavior. People seem ready and willing for the introduction of new policies that guide them to change their behavior in favor of climate change challenges. They are hoping that the government will make it easier for them to act sustainably.

2. **Focus on behavior.** Policy action needs to be grounded in an understanding and awareness of consumer behavior. At the same time, there exists a need to identify and set priorities around the behaviors that need to be encouraged or sustained. For example, people need to see symbolic and effective solutions in their everyday lives to be encouraged to act more sustainably. Some actions create a stronger commitment to sustainability than the action itself, rippling outwards by opening people's minds to different ways of doing things.

3. **Place products and services at the centre**. Collaborative partnerships between business and government are critical to make sustainable products and services the norm. It is crucial that policy-makers set long-term sustainability 'roadmaps' for products and services to drive the evolution of the industry towards sustainability.

4. **Build collective actions.** The role of governments is to facilitate collective responses to collective problems that cannot be solved by individual choice. It is extremely hard to deviate widely from the collective norms individually. In other words, governments should act as a collective action facilitator to help people solve shared problems.

5. **Widen the mandate.** Along with the progress, it is recommended to change and foster the mandate. Interruptions to reflect further action are appropriate, as this can help to resolve many complex challenges. After all, there are many tensions, trade-offs and dilemmas at the heart of such a complex challenge as sustainable consumption.

> ## *Implementation of 4E's strategy in the UK.*
>
> In 2005, the government signed up for a Sustainable Development Strategy based on the four Es – Exemplify, Enable, Encourage and Engage people and communities in the move towards sustainability. The government recognized the need to lead by example and make interventions tangible, fair and the norm [90].
>
> The strategy of the government emphasized that engagement requires a real commitment to community action, deliberative processes and involving people in changing the perspective on their own terms. This is seen as better than a one-way process of communicating and relying on conventional persuasion.
>
> An example of the achievements of the strategy put in practice was London's congestion charge. A combination of charging, combined with the increased provision of buses, was introduced with accompanying publicity. The effects have been far greater than originally forecast. There has been a 30% reduction in congestion as people consider alternatives, including public transport, with an increase of 29,000 bus passengers entering the zone in the morning peak times.

Enable
-Remove barriers
-Give information
-Provide facilities
-Provide viable alternatives
-Educate/ train/ provide skills
-Provide capacity

4E's STRATEGY

Encourage
-Tax system
-Expenditure- grants
-Reward schemes
-Recognition / social
pressure- league tables
-Penalties, fines and
enforcement action

Engage
-Community action
-Co-production
-Deliberative form
-Personal contacts/
enthusiasts
-Media campaigns/
opinion formers
-Use network

Exemplify
-Leading by example
-Achieving consistency
in policies

Similarly, the Swedish government is taking systemic actions to promote sustainable consumption and production transition. The government's strategy for sustainable consumption aims to contribute to environmentally, socially and economically sustainable consumption focusing on these main areas:
Increasing knowledge and deepening cooperation, encouraging sustainable ways of consuming, streamlining resource use, improving information on companies' sustainability efforts, phasing out harmful chemicals, improving security for all consumers and focusing on food, transport and housing [32].

The role of governments must be to stimulate, in a supervisory and legislative way, sustainable consumption and production in both business and citizens. Through policies and public awareness, governments can influence consumer habits and production processes towards sustainable actions.

Business

Businesses as providers of products and services play a critical role in the creation of more sustainable innovation. <u>Businesses that are prepared to make strategic low-carbon actions and provide sustainable services and products have the opportunity to shape and lead the market.</u> By setting a trend, competitors and other sectors of the market will consequently tend to follow where they see a business case to finally achieve global transformation of the market.

On the one hand, businesses will have to choose new corporate responsibility towards sustainable consumption. In order to do so, the businesses' approach should implement the following principles:

• Make the transformation of their business strategy evident with new principles of sustainable consumption.

• Analyze the environmental and social impacts on the entire life cycle of interventions.

• Have proactive engagement with the government and NGOs to develop public policies that stimulate more sustainable products.

• Research and develop strategies focused on product sustainability.

• Design features that help consumers use their products or services in more sustainable ways.

• Implement marketing strategies that appeal to people's values and ethics, and a broader sense of well-being, and avoid creating new unnecessary and unsustainable wants.

• Create partnerships with innovative enterprises to develop more sustainable products or service approaches.

On the other hand, businesses must also have a coherent and sustainable supply chain. This helps to ensure continued improvement of stakeholder value. By achieving a reduction of resource use from the supply chain, such as energy, water or materials, there will be significant cost savings.

These savings can be transferred to consumers and can reduce the product cost, which helps in reaching a mainstream population, rather than only offering expensive, luxurious and unaffordable products to small and wealthy markets.
There is an opportunity to promote business stability and innovate by being proactive towards governmental priorities and by operating efficiently within regulatory boundaries. This gives businesses the opportunity to influence the policy agenda in the increasing movement of environmental regulations for climate protection all around the world.

Likewise, while encouraging sustainability outwards, it is also essential to pass the sustainable values inwards to employees and potential employees, in order to increase morale and efficiency. This will create satisfaction and attraction in employees to help society meet its aspirations of responsible and sustainable behavior.
In other words, sustainability should be embedded in the culture, philosophy and values of every single cell of the business, both inwards and outwards.

Businesses that are prepared to make strategic low-carbon actions and provide sustainable services and products have the opportunity to shape and lead the market.

People

One of the biggest challenges of sustainable development is to reach the mainstream population. In 2004, fewer than one in three people had heard the term 'sustainable development' and even fewer of that group could explain what it means [18].

For a sustainable future, it is necessary to involve consumers more and raise awareness about the connection of their daily choices and the consequences in the world around them.

Changes in the production of goods and services cannot do all the heavy lifting necessary to make the sustainable consumption and production transition. Changes in the attitudes, values and behavior of consumers matter too. More consumers who care about their carbon, water and land footprints and about what happens at the far end of long supply chains – and who make their purchasing decisions accordingly - are indeed essential.

Consumers' daily choices and behaviors have a major fundamental impact on the environment in four main areas:

MAIN AREAS OF OUR DAILY LIFE WITH MAJOR IMPACT

Food

Energy and Water consumption

Long distance mobility

Short distance mobility

- How we manage our homes (energy and water consumption)
- The food we consume (food)
- How we get around (short-distance mobility)
- Holiday or business travels (long-distance mobility)

Greater awareness and responsibility among consumers about their everyday consumption patterns can put pressure on producers to move their own operations and their suppliers towards sustainability and simultaneously give politicians and governments the political space to enact the regulations, policies and market instruments that drive society towards a sustainable future.

The Forum [79] provided four key guidelines that can be applied both by businesses and by the government to make sustainable habits and choices easier for those consumers who choose to take action in these areas:

1. **Make it fair.** Consumers are highly motivated to contribute to global fairness with the products and services they consume. However, people want to be sure that interventions are fair and not open to abuse by free riders or manipulation by 'rich' people [36, 6]. When the polluter pays in equal proportion for their negative impact, consumers perceive the intervention as being fair.

2. **Help people act together.** People want assurance that, with their behavior, they would be acting in collaboration rather than isolation. To make interventions that prompt new behaviors, they need to become 'social norms' to be truly effective and successful [35,40].

3. **Make it positive and tangible.** People get more engaged when they can see the positive consequences of their choices, rather than the negative impact. People like to do (and make visible to everyone) positive and tangible actions.

4. **Win the trust of people.** Transparency helps to overcome the normal tendency of people to be skeptical about the motives of the government and businesses. Above all, interventions need to communicate that they are motivated by environmental concerns, rather than the economic interest of raising revenue. Likewise, businesses and governments should promote sustainability not only with the interventions created for people, but also by having sustainability as a core of their corporate identity and setting the example with their own acts and internal processes.

To achieve community action and consequently a great positive impact and change, real individual engagement and the commitment of consumers is required. Therefore, it is imperative to utilize deliberative processes that involve people in changing their perspective on their own terms. This, above all, is due to their great power to influence the market and change consumption and production patterns. This is why it should not just be a one-way process of communicating and relying on conventional persuasion, but rather an integral approach to eliminate barriers and ensure that consumers get informed, choose, consume and behave more sustainably.

Barriers to sustainable consumer choice

Consumers play a major role in making products and services more sustainable. Their choices have a great impact on which goods exist on the market. Their behavior determines when, how, where and what is being produced. Besides regulations, market forces are a major driver in the way industries develop. Consumers can now demand new standards for corporate behavior and a higher commitment towards the purpose of producing more sustainably, not just making a profit. This means that by buying and consuming, consumers can 'reward' more sustainable services and products, or 'punish' less sustainable alternatives. This gives great power to consumers to create a breakpoint in the chain and influence the market and the industry about what and how is being produced.

One major problem is that sustainability is a broad and abstract concept with many definitions, and it is not clear for many people. In general, consumers perceive sustainability as a positive thing and may have a forward-looking attitude towards central components of sustainability, such as environmental protection; however, there is a high tendency towards the intention-behavior gap.

Acting positively towards sustainability and buying less sustainable products or services is not necessarily a contradiction. For instance, in the UK, 30% of people claim to care about companies' environmental and social records, but only 3% reflect this in their purchases [17].

The fact that the sustainability of a service or product cannot always be checked by consumers, as it cannot be seen, tasted or felt if it has been produced in a more sustainable way, often makes it difficult to make decisions towards sustainable options. For this reason, sustainability turns into a reliance characteristic of goods and trustful relations with the brands and industries consumers choose.

Therefore, making a clear and comprehensible communication strategy of the sustainable aspects of goods is crucial. Lately, eco-labeling – the transmission of sustainable information on the label – has been used more and more for this purpose [23]. There are many kinds of eco-labels on products, services and processes that mostly cover certain aspects of the broad sustainability concept. Some of the most known and used labels designate the carbon footprint, local production, organic production, environmental protection, fair trade, animal welfare and other aspects of the production process, as well as the origin of raw materials.

However, eco-labeling and informative efforts are not enough to persuade consumers to act more sustainably. There are a number of frequent barriers in the decision-making and purchase process that can be prevented to affect consumer choice, which will encourage more sustainable alternatives to be chosen above others in the marketplace.

Klaus Grunert [33] points out six barriers to sustainable consumer food choice that can also be transposed and applied to different goods in different sectors with sustainable labels and information. He exposes the reasons why a consumer might not choose a more sustainable option, or not make such an option a recurrent choice. To influence consumer choice based on the sustainability of the intervention, consumers need to perceive the sustainable aspects, attach some form of understanding to them, and decide what these aspects mean for them. They need to be aware of their decision making, to ensure that the sustainability will not be traded off against other criteria.

The whole process is affected by whether consumers are aware of the sustainable aspects, label, information provided and if they find it credible. It also depends on their values and intention towards sustainability. This must be translated into motivation to choose sustainable options at the time of decision-making and purchase. Based on this framework, Klaus G. concludes his work with the following six possible barriers:

1. **Exposure does not lead to perception.** Consumers simply do not notice the label, because they are time-pressured when shopping and most purchases are made habitually.

2. **Perception leads only to peripheral processing.** Consumers see the label, but do not care to make the effort to understand what it means. It may still affect their choices, though.

3. **Consumers make 'wrong' inferences.** Consumers do see the label, make an effort to understand what it means, but draw the wrong inferences. They may end up buying the product, but may do so for the 'wrong' reasons.

4. **Eco-information is traded off against other criteria.** Consumers prioritize other aspects of the product over sustainability. The price may be higher, the taste is not as good, the rest of the family prefers something else, etc.

5. **Lack of awareness and/or credibility.** Consumers who want to make sustainable choices may find it hard to carry them out in practice.

6. **Lack of motivation at time of choice.** While consumers have a positive attitude towards sustainability, this attitude is not strong enough to affect behavior in all situations where sustainability may be a criterion. We can say that consumers 'forget' about their positive attitude regarding sustainability when making choices. Such 'dormant' attitudes are a major factor in explaining discrepancies between attitude and behavior.

These barriers can be translated and applied not only to eco-labeling, but also as general barriers to sustainable consumption at the moment of making a choice whenever the consumer is about to buy or decide between a sustainable alternative and a less sustainable one. The barriers can occur when people gain information about a product themselves, when buying online, or when they are persuaded by word-of-mouth marketing strategies. All of these occur without having any contact with the label.

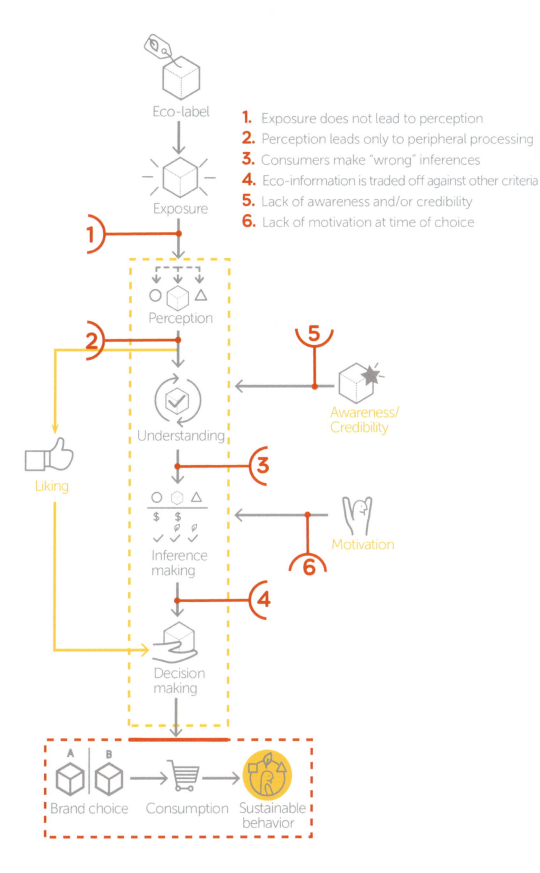

1. Exposure does not lead to perception
2. Perception leads only to peripheral processing
3. Consumers make "wrong" inferences
4. Eco-information is traded off against other criteria
5. Lack of awareness and/or credibility
6. Lack of motivation at time of choice

Eco-label

Exposure

Perception

Understanding

Awareness/
Credibility

Liking

Inference
making

Motivation

Decision
making

Brand choice   Consumption   Sustainable
behavior

CONSUMERS, BEHAVIOR AND HABITS

BASICS

Consumption is a broader activity that, besides purchasing, is also reflected in rituals of use and concrete or symbolic modification of goods. Products and services acting as interfaces between consumers and consumption activities give immediate and direct responses to users when being operated: perception, learning process and use. Designing a service means, among many others, designing a user experience that determines the compound impacts of it and how future decisions are made.

In order to make consumers perform a planned sustainable behavior, it is crucial to have a better understanding of what they do, and how they interact with products and services, as well as the hidden factors behind their daily decision-making process.
In recent decades, many theories have tried to explain the factors that contribute to behavioral change. For instance, Triandis [85] proposed an integrated model of interpersonal behavior that includes social factors and emotions in forming intentions. It also highlights the importance of habits as a mediated factor related to behavioral change.

Jackson [40] states that a behavior only becomes habitual when the behavior is 'highly automated,' meaning that the behavior is performed with minimum cognitive effort, resulting in limited awareness during the interaction. Grabbing our usual brand of detergent in the supermarket, following a specific route when traveling to work and drinking coffee in the morning to start the day are habitual behaviors; what they have in common is that they are performed with a minimum amount of thinking.

Habits, as defined by Verplanken and Aarts (cited by Verplanken and Wood [101]) "are learned sequences of acts that have become automatic responses to specific cues, and are functional in obtaining certain goals or end-states." In other words, habits are actions learned and performed as a routine to achieve a specific goal, for instance, always turning off the lights after leaving the room to lower the energy bill. There are three stages in the formation of a new habit: [2, 63]

1. **The declarative stage:** the individual encodes information relevant to the behavior as a set of facts.

2. **The knowledge compilation stage:** the information is converted from declarative to procedural and conscious attention to the information is gradually reduced.

3. **The final procedural stage:** the habit is formed and performed with lower amounts of attention.

Many unsustainable behaviors are habits rather than active choices. In order to encourage consumers to break old habits, two factors are suggested: repetition and reinforcement. To make people break a habit in the first place, it is critical to understand who they are, why they behave the way they do, and most importantly, why and how the old habit was formed.

It is indeed important to create consistent behaviors over time that can lead to sustainable habits. Mainstreaming sustainability starts with creating sustainable habits. This could be the key to a truly sustainable future.

To influence consumer choice based on the sustainability of the intervention, consumers need to perceive the sustainable aspects, attach some form of understanding to them, and decide what these aspects mean for them.

Consumer types and characteristics

When designing an intervention, product or service, it is important to define the target users (consumers to perform the new behavior), because everyone is in a different life stage, which affects their behavioral and decision-making processes.
The Sinus Milieus [71] are presented within a social and target group model that groups people according to their lifestyles and values. It shows the very different proportions of the population represented by each milieu (sections of the population with a similar socio-cultural background). However, the boundaries between the milieus are fluid. There are also areas of contact and transition between the milieus. The two axes for the classification are 1) how traditional their basic values are and 2) the social value, which is measured by the level of education, income and occupational group of its members.
This exemplifies that consumers are clearly not a homogenous group.
Societies are composed of sociocultural diversity with different sensitivities and orientations, values, life goals, lifestyles, attitudes and social backgrounds.
Due to this socio-cultural diversity, people might respond to the same intervention

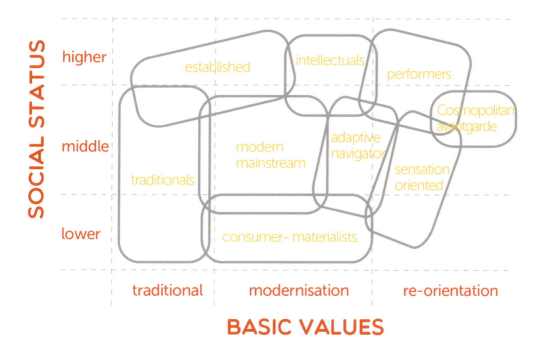

Graphic based on Sinus- Meta Milieus for established markets 2017

strategy in very different ways. For instance, it may lead some consumers to a behavior change, but this might not be applicable to others.

The explanation for this is that the effect of behavioral determinants (e.g. economic, social, or environmental factors that influence the behavior) varies across individuals [20, 53, 74]. Consequently, when designing sustainable interventions to change consumer behavior, it is indeed crucial to know which behaviors and which behavioral factors should be addressed to achieve this change. Applied to our problem here, this means that in order to create a successful intervention and persuade the target audience to choose pro-environmental behavior, the persuasive systems should be designed according to an in-depth exploration of the target users, generating a direct correspondence with their different needs.

Within a sustainable consumption context, consumers can be classified in clusters based on sustainable consumption acceptance, perception, intention and performance.

The segments can be clustered on two axes: attitude and behavioral intention towards sustainability. As a result, four different consumer types can be proposed [99,14]: irresponsible consumers, undecided consumers, worried consumers and enthusiastic consumers. Worried and undecided consumers display conflicting attitudes and behavior intention, and represent the majority of the population with an intention-behavior gap.

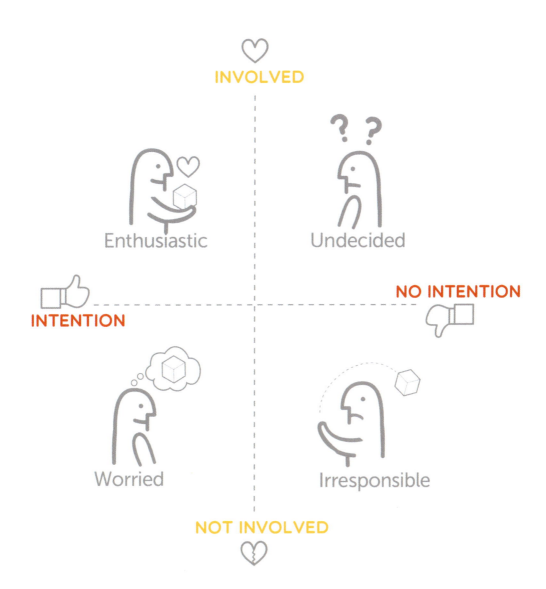

Enthusiastic consumers

Enthusiastic consumers are those of the opinion that it is very positive and meaningful to buy sustainable products and are involved with sustainable consumption. This consumer segment has already performed (and perhaps is still performing) pro-environmental behaviors. They tend to be very sensitive towards environmental topics and issues. These consumers believe that their choices mean a lot for the environment (regarding the importance of performing individual eco-friendly behaviors) and for other people. However, their performance of pro-environmental behaviors may not be repetitive due to motivation that weakens or disappears, or because of the emergence of a new barrier, such as time or money constraints.

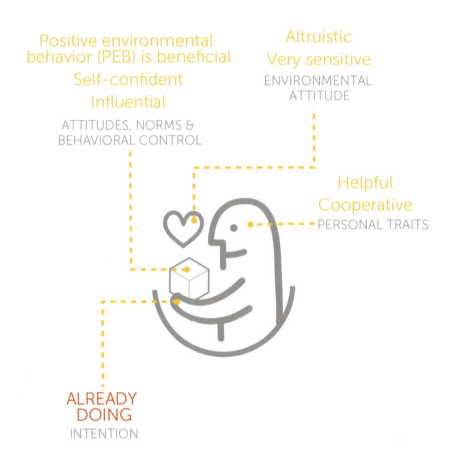

Positive environmental behavior (PEB) is beneficial
Self-confident
Influential
ATTITUDES, NORMS & BEHAVIORAL CONTROL

Altruistic
Very sensitive
ENVIRONMENTAL ATTITUDE

Helpful
Cooperative
PERSONAL TRAITS

ALREADY DOING
INTENTION

Irresponsible consumers

These are consumers who do not have a positive attitude towards sustainable products nor do they have the intention of buying them, and are therefore less involved with sustainable consumption. Irresponsible consumers tend to be egocentric, have no concern for environmental issues and do not feel responsible for environmental problems. They have a neutral position on the perception of consumer effectiveness. The most effective strategy would be to change these consumers' values from an emphasis on power and authority to striving for a better world, but this long-term goal would be hard to realize.

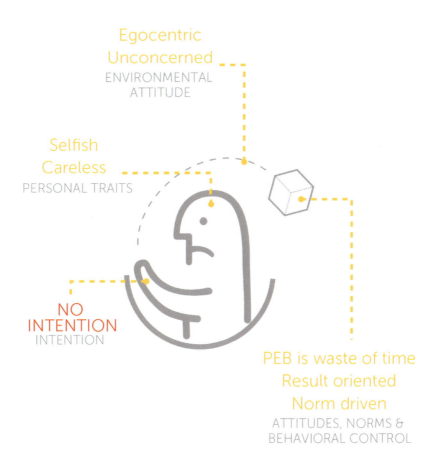

Egocentric
Unconcerned
ENVIRONMENTAL
ATTITUDE

Selfish
Careless
PERSONAL TRAITS

NO
INTENTION
INTENTION

PEB is waste of time
Result oriented
Norm driven
ATTITUDES, NORMS &
BEHAVIORAL CONTROL

Worried consumers

This segment consists of consumers that have a positive environmental behavior (PEB) and therefore a positive attitude towards sustainable products and generally feel responsible for environmental problems. They are concerned about the well-being of future generations. However, they do not have the intention to perform pro-environmental behaviors for several reasons. First, they are routine-oriented and are not open to change their routines. Second, they might have misbeliefs about sustainable products and services—for example, if they are not available in their neighborhood or surroundings. Finally, they struggle to understand or use these services and products effectively.

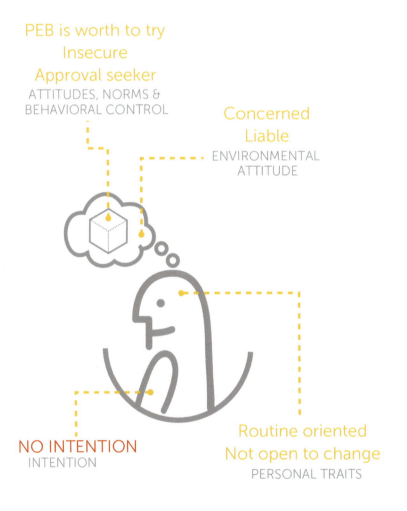

PEB is worth to try
Insecure
Approval seeker
ATTITUDES, NORMS &
BEHAVIORAL CONTROL

Concerned
Liable
ENVIRONMENTAL
ATTITUDE

NO INTENTION
INTENTION

Routine oriented
Not open to change
PERSONAL TRAITS

Undecided consumers

This segment corresponds to consumers who do not feel positive about sustainable products, but nevertheless claim that it is very likely they will buy these products. This inconsistency can be understood by their belief about social norms. Undecided consumers generally feel responsible for environmental problems, but they appear to be confused about whether their actions can change the situation. Even so, they want to know how to decrease their negative impact on the environment, but are reluctant to act due to the lack of sufficient knowledge and behavioral control. These consumers tend to act because their friends and family find it fairly important that they buy sustainable products.

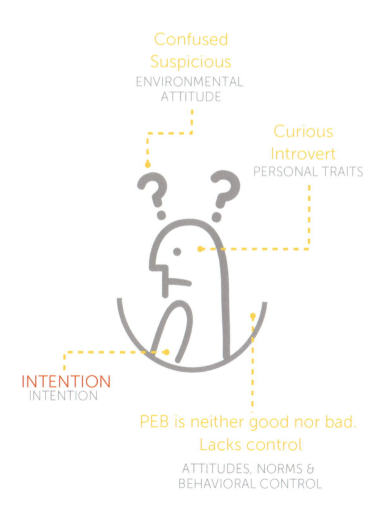

Confused
Suspicious
ENVIRONMENTAL
ATTITUDE

Curious
Introvert
PERSONAL TRAITS

INTENTION
INTENTION

PEB is neither good nor bad.
Lacks control

ATTITUDES, NORMS &
BEHAVIORAL CONTROL

The four consumer types have different environmental attitudes, personalities, levels of behavioral control and opinions regarding the impact of positive environmental behavior. Consequently, the methods for approaching and reaching them have the most potential when the intervention matches their attitudes and personality, and communicates this through the configuration characteristics.

This categorization is an example of the macro level of consumer types, but lacks an in-depth explanation of specific consumer behaviors, goals and thoughts, which can provide valuable input for designers when planning and designing an intervention. This can be overcome by conducting further research about the particular target consumer.
The ROADMAP section explains in depth how each consumer cluster can be influenced to be more sustainable through different design interventions and facilitator strategies.

	Environmental attitude	Personality traits	Attitudes, norms and behavioral control	Intention
Enthusiastic	Altruistic Very sensitive	Helpful Cooperative	PEB is beneficial Self-confident Influential	ALREADY DOING
Irresponsible	Egocentric Unconcerned	Selfish Careless	PEB is a waste of time Result oriented Norm driven	NO
Worried	Concerned Liable	Routine oriented Not open to change	PEB is worth to try Insecure Approval seeker	YES
Undecided	Confused Suspicious	Curious Introvert	PEB is neither good nor bad Lacks control	NO

Factors influencing consumer behavior towards sustainability

According to BJ Fogg, every behavior is a product of three elements: motivation, ability and prompts. This means that for a person to perform a behavior, that person must firstly be sufficiently motivated, secondly, they must have the ability to perform it, and finally, they must be prompted to perform the behavior. These three factors must occur at the same moment, or else the behavior will not occur [27].

In most cases, persuasive technologies boost motivation or ability, but this is not enough. The behavior must be prompted in order to be performed.

Motivation

Motivation is a state that energizes, directs and sustains a behavior. It involves goals and requires actions. Goals provide the impulse to make an action and the direction of the action. At the same time, actions require effort in terms of persistence to sustain an activity for a long period of time. Thus, to convince consumers to perform a behavior, motivation is imperative.

According to the Fogg Behavior Model (FBM) [27], there are three core motivator pairs that can be used to boost the motivation to perform a behavior:

1. **Pleasure/Pain:** The result of these motivators is usually immediate, or nearly so. There is little thinking or anticipation involved. People are responding to what is happening in the given moment.

2. **Hope/Fear:** These motivators are characterized by the anticipation of an outcome. Hope is the anticipation of something good happening and fear is the anticipation of something bad, often loss or failure.

3. **Social acceptance/Rejection:** People are motivated to perform certain behaviors in order to be socially accepted. This desire is even more present to avoid being rejected by others. Nowadays, this dimension controls much of our social behavior.

Ability

People need to have the ability required to perform a behavior. Particularly in new behaviors, this could be a decisive point. It determines if the consumer accepts or rejects the opportunity to act.

However, teaching and training consumers to behave differently or in a more complex way demands effort. Consumers tend to be resistant, since it requires time, energy and sometimes money to change their behavior.

Thus, designers should increase the ability of consumers by making a given task easy or easier to accomplish. In other words, to increase the ability relies heavily on the power of simplicity in the product, service or intervention, besides being price

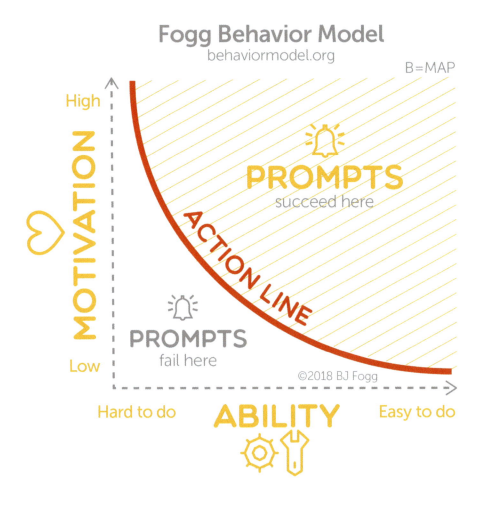

Graphic based on Fogg Behavior Model [27]

competitive and not scarce. According to Fogg, the success or failure of simplifying depends heavily on a series of six elements. It is important to note that one negatively affected element dramatically increases the chance of failure:

1. **Time:** If a target behavior requires time and the consumer doesn't have time available, then the behavior is not simple to perform.

2. **Money:** For people with limited financial resources, a target behavior that costs money is not suitable to perform.

3. **Physical effort:** Behaviors that require a certain physical effort might not be simple enough to perform.

4. **Brain cycles:** Behavior that requires people to think hard might not be simple. This is especially the case when the mind is focused on other topics.

5. **Social deviance:** This means going against the norm and breaking the rules of society. If a behavior requires one to be socially deviant, that behavior is no longer appropriate to perform.

6. **Non-routine:** People tend to find behaviors simple if they are routine. When people face a behavior that is not routine, they might not want to make that effort.

Prompts

Prompts can also be called triggers, cues, calls to action and so on, but the ideas are all similar. A prompt is something that tells people to perform a behavior at a given moment.

Successful prompts have three characteristics: The prompt is perceived, associated with a target behavior, and both of those happen when the person is motivated and able to perform the behavior.

Prompts can be clustered into three types related to the degree of motivation and ability:

1. **Spark:** The prompt is designed with a motivational element for a person that lacks the motivation to perform a target behavior.

2. **Facilitator:** This makes the behavior easier. This type of prompt is appropriate for users that have high motivation, but lack the ability. The goal of a facilitator is to prompt the behavior, while also making it easier to follow.

3. **Signal:** This prompt indicates or reminds. It works best when people have both the ability and the motivation to act. The signal does not seek to motivate people or simplify the task; it simply works as a reminder.

Additionally, there are other parallel factors that influence sustainable consumer behavior across motivation, ability and prompts. According to Stern[74], there are four major types of causal variables that affect environmentally significant behavior.

- Attitudinal factors
- External or contextual forces
- Personal capabilities
- Behaviors that occur as habit or routine

Rural Afghan girl Vs. NY City girl

As Lucie Evers, a Dutch marketeer for sustainability and social entrepreneur, once said to me, reaffirming the factors that influence consumer behavior, "Both a teenage girl in the mountains of Afghanistan with an IQ of 136 who only has the Koran as a study book, and a girl of the same age who is born in New York with the same IQ, but whose parents are both lawyers, have different constraints coming from the contextual and social forces, personal capabilities, and routines that will influence and define their behavior and decision-making process at every level."

This example illustrates that consumer choice is circumscribed by the conditioned variety of forces and constraints in complex social, economic, institutional and technological systems, and consequently, the environmental impact of their choice.

Following the example, the girl from Afghanistan, if willing to make green choices, may find limited options and costs prohibitive due to a lack of relevant products or infrastructure. However, due to the local conditions, it is more likely that the lifestyle in the mountains of Afghanistan is less consumerist and that solutions are adapted to local circumstances and basic needs. Hence, the economy is more locally oriented and, consequently, the environmental impact is relatively low.

In contrast is the case of the girl from New York. Willing to make green choices, she might find information more easily, as well as a variety of options and products, while money would not be a relevant constraint. Nonetheless, as is generally the case in the United States, the lifestyle based on the capitalist economic system and the high amount of petroleum-derived options in the market limits the potential for environmental improvement because of the difficulty of acquiring trustworthy and timely information about the environmental consequences of decisions. Even so, an increasing number of products and services are marketed with claims that they are environmentally benign or beneficial.

Therefore, all these final factors, as well as the motivation, ability and prompts, must be taken into consideration when facing the challenge of designing an intervention that promotes behavioral change. Only this approach can ensure that the behavior is possible and simple to perform by consumers.

FACTORS
INFLUENCING

External environment

Structural trends in society
individualisation
increased personal mobility

**Contextual environment
& infrastructure**
social, political, economic,
cultural, technological

Social environment
family, friends, colleagues, others

Personal capabilities
knowledge
skills
social status
finance

Internal Factors

Attitudinal factors
environmental &
non-environmental orientation
clashing & complementing

Habits & Routines

Life events

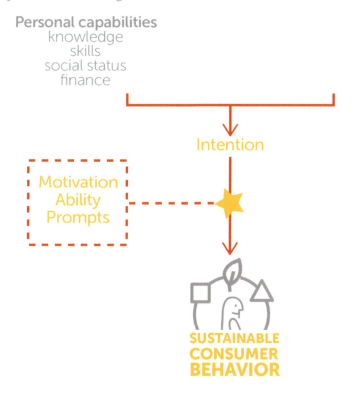

Intention

Motivation
Ability
Prompts

**SUSTAINABLE
CONSUMER
BEHAVIOR**

STRATEGIES TO DESIGN SUSTAINABLE CONSUMER BEHAVIOR

BASICS

As stated in earlier chapters, consumers constantly make choices that do not always support their long-term sustainable goals or ethical values (intention-behavior gap). This effect is explained through psychology theories by the fact that our brain works on two different levels: automatic and reflective [30].

On the one hand, automatic thinking is very energy effective and bases the judgments on a preset of biases and previous experiences. It happens quickly and without dependence on our awareness to react. This kind of thinking bases the decisions on our subconscious urges and needs. It does not give the right value and rational thinking to long-term goals and ethical values.
Reflective thinking, on the other hand, is based on rational reflections, and uses our cognitive abilities to understand and consider situations before reacting and responding to them.

Automatic thinking is what our brain tends to rely on the most for our daily life, because reflective thinking demands much more energy and attention, and our bodies are biologically wired to save as much energy as possible.
In order to convert their (persuasive) intentions into interventions to promote more sustainable consumer behavior, designers must consider the way the human cognitive system works on these two levels.

Notwithstanding, designers have this ability and can communicate persuasive arguments to users. These intentions can have positive or negative consequences and may affect behavior change both intentionally and unintentionally.
Design for behavior change acknowledges this capacity and responsibility of designers and attempts to facilitate a shift in the everyday choices of the population.
DfBC aims to create positive change to close the so-called intention-behavior gap between people's attitudes (which are often pro-environmental) and their everyday behavior.

Automatic   VS.   Reflective

THINKING

Energy effective	⚡	Energy consuming
Based on preset of biases and previous experiences	? → !	Based on rational reflections
Quick	🕐	Time consuming
No awareness needed to react. Based on subconscious urges and needs	💭	Use of cognitive abilities to understand and consider situations before reacting and responding

Consumer behavior change strategies

The consumer attitude towards an intervention can be changed by making a particular need important. A key aspect in changing attitudes and behaviors is to use the functional approach, the function of mental processes involving consciousness, in utilitarian (utility function of the intervention), ego-defensive (protect themselves and feel secure and safe about the intervention), value-expressive (expression or reflection of the consumer's general values) and knowledge functions (knowing more about the intervention) [70].

Furthermore, another key aspect is the importance for consumers to see that the desired behavior and attitude towards the intervention is really not in conflict with another personal behavior or belief. This can sometimes resolve actual or potential conflicts between two attitudes and may be induced to change their evaluation of the attitude and perform the desired behavior.

Based on the factors that influence consumer behavior and the two levels of the human cognitive system, consumption patterns can be altered with the application of strategies embedded in the intervention. Two of them are illustrated below. They can be used to reinforce the two key aspects mentioned before and ensure consumer behavior change.

NUDGING

The term 'nudge' means a gentle push or touch. The Nudge Method attempts to do exactly that: to gently push people in a preferable direction. Nudging, as a method, aims to create predictable behavioral outcomes based on how the human brain perceives the world and makes decisions. Thaler and Sunstein [82] set the original definition of nudging as "any aspect of the choice architecture that alters people's behavior in a predictable way without forbidding any options or significantly changing their economic incentives."

Using nudging strategies, policy makers and industries have the opportunity to alter the behavior of people in ways that simultaneously benefit both the user and society as a whole.

Designers acting as mediators of the touch points between the interventions and the consumers can engrave implicit nudges in the design to affect consumer behavior in both automatic and reflective ways, and to also understand the reasoning behind how the choices are made.

Cass R. Sunstein [12] compiled a list of various nudge techniques and some simple examples:

- **Default rules:** Nudges that automatically enroll people in the action, like setting people in a specific program, such as default double-sided printing in university printers. Default rules may be the most effective nudges and can promote environmental protection. They are indispensable, especially when it is too burdensome and time-consuming for people to choose.

Default rules ------ Simplification ------ Use of social norms

Increase in ease & convenience ------ Disclosure ------ Warnings

Pre- commitment strategies ------ Reminder ------ Eliciting implementation intentions

- **Simplification:** Simplifies information in order to facilitate and avoid misunderstandings and make complex inferences more intuitive. In both rich and poor countries, complexity is a serious problem because it causes confusion, increases costs, and deters participation in important actions. As a general rule, interventions should be easy to follow or even intuitive.

- **Use of social norms:** Emphasizing what most people are doing is an effective nudge to engage people in a certain behavior (e.g., "most of your coworkers are doing car-sharing" or "nine out of ten hotel guests reuse their towels").
  It is indeed effective to inform people that others are engaged in a certain behavior. Such information is often most powerful when it is as local and specific as possible (e.g., "the overwhelming majority of people in your community have reduced their car use by fifty percent").

- **Increase in ease and convenience:** This type of nudge aims to make things easy. For instance, making organic and local food more visible in supermarkets will increase the possibility of it being picked. People often make the easy choice, thus reducing various barriers (including the time it takes to understand what to do) is often helpful. A supplemental point: If the easy choice is also fun, people are more likely to make it.

- **Disclosure:** Make information accessible; for example: by demonstrating the positive or neutral environmental impact of sustainable and fair clothing on their labels and in their marketing strategies. Disclosure nudges can be highly effective, particularly if the information is both comprehensible and accessible. Simplicity is exceedingly important (e.g., "More detailed and fuller disclosure might be made available online for those who are interested in it").

- **Warnings, graphics or otherwise:** Nudges can also be more explicit in describing the risks of some behavior, like the warnings found on cigarette packaging. If serious risks are involved, the best nudge might be a warning. A central point is that attention is a scarce resource, and warnings are attentive to that fact. Research also shows that people are far less likely to discount a warning when it is accompanied by a description of the concrete steps that people can take to reduce the relevant risk (e.g., "You can do X and Y to lower your risk").

- **Pre-commitment strategies:** To encourage people to engage in a specific course of action to reach their goals. People often have certain objectives, like supporting animal activism and not consuming animal-based products. However, their behavior falls short of those goals. If people pre-commit to engage in a certain action, such as signing a petition for animal cruelty-free products and reminding them of their decision, they are more likely to act in accordance with their goals. Notably, committing to a specific action at a precise future moment in time motivates action and reduces procrastination.

- **Reminders:** To avoid procrastination or forgetfulness, a reminder can have a significant impact. People can be nudged by being alerted of their upcoming obligations or commitments, such as by email or text message. With reminders, timing greatly matters; making sure that people can act immediately on the information is critical (especially in light of the occasional tendency towards forgetfulness).

- **Eliciting implementation intentions:** When asked about their intention to engage in a certain activity, people are more likely to do so (e.g., "Do you really want to use a plastic straw?").

THE BEHAVIOR WIZARD

Fogg and his Stanford team created a tool called the Behavior Wizard. It categorizes behaviors into 15 types [2]. The tool is composed of a grid formed by the horizontal axis as a dimension called the 'behavior flavor' (five flavors) and the vertical axis, which maps out the 'duration' (three durations).

Behavior Flavors

- **Green (non-familiar/new behavior)** is a type of behavior that is new to the target audience. To design an intervention to achieve a Green Behavior requires special consideration. This may include making the behavior simpler, reducing anxiety, connecting the new behavior to existing practices, providing social support, etc.

- **Blue (familiar behavior)** is a behavior that the target audience is already familiar with. For example, having breakfast is a Blue Behavior for most people. To achieve these behaviors, designers can draw on past experiences. Over time, a Green Behavior turns into a Blue Behavior as a person becomes more familiar with it.

- **Purple (increase behavior)** is the increased performance of a familiar behavior. These behaviors are already performed and the aim is to increase them in some way, such as performing the behavior for longer, more intensely, or with more effort.

- **Gray (decrease behavior)** designates a decrease in the performance of a familiar behavior. The behavior can decrease in intensity, duration, or frequency, such as using fewer palm oil products, consuming less energy at home, or buying fewer plastic products.

- **Black (stop behavior)** designates the cessation of an existing behavior. For example, ceasing to eat meat is a black behavior.

Durations of Behaviors

- **Dot Behavior** is a behavior that is done only once.

- **Span Behavior** is a behavior that is done over a period of time. For example, you could substitute rice for quinoa for one month. Designing Span Behaviors requires special consideration, as people must stick to a pattern of action for a certain period of time. Thus, a Span intervention may need regular prompts.

- **Path Behavior** is a behavior that is done from now on for the foreseeable future.

This is a permanent change. For example, becoming a permanent vegetarian is an example of this behavior. Path Behaviors may be the hardest types of behaviors to induce. Due to their permanent nature, they require a significant and lasting shift in a person's identity or lifestyle. In many cases, the target behavior must be prompted regularly enough to the point that the behavior becomes a habit, part of a person's routine or a reflexive response.

Each of these 15 behavior types requires different psychological strategies and persuasive techniques to reach the targeted behavior.
In the next section, ROADMAP, the strategies for each of them will be explained in depth.

Fogg Behavior Grid

behaviorgrid.org

	Dot · is done one-time	Span ⊢ has specific duration such as 40 days	Path → is done from now on, a permanent change
Green Do new behavior, one that is unfamiliar	**Green Dot** Do new behavior, one time *Instal solar panels at home*	**Green Span** Do new behavior, for a period of time *Carpool to work for three weeks*	**Green Path** Do new behavior from now on *Start growing own vegetables*
Blue Do familiar behavior	**Blue Dot** Do familiar behavior one time *Plant a tree*	**Blue Span** Do familiar behavior for a period of time *Bike to work for two months*	**Blue Path** Do familiar behavior from now on *Turn off light when leaving the room*
Purple Increase behavior intensity or duration	**Purple Dot** Increase behavior one time *Buy today more vegetables than meat*	**Purple Span** Increase behavior for a period of time *Use more public bus for one month*	**Purple Path** Increase behavior from now on *Purchase more local products*
Gray Decrease behavior intensity or duration	**Gray Dot** Decrease behavior one time *Use less detergent for the laudry today*	**Gray Span** Decrease behavior for a period of time *Take shorter showers this week*	**Gray Path** Decrease behavior from now on *Eat less palm oil products from now on*
Black Stop doing a behavior	**Black Dot** Stop a behavior one time *Turn off the heater tonight*	**Black Span** Stop a behavior for a period of time *Don't water lawn during spring*	**Black Path** Stop a behavior from now on *Never eat meat again, become vegetarian*

Graphic based on Fogg. BJ. BEHAVIOR GRID
www.behaviorwizard.org

Sustainable design strategies

The term sustainable design has been used in multiple disciplines and refers to a design process that integrates an environmentally-friendly approach that considers natural resources as an essential part of the design.
Sustainable design acts as a philosophy to achieve a better future for the human race through the wise and reduced consumption of Earth's resources.
This approach is applied by different companies, governmental entities, and non-governmental organizations. Companies and governments with leading design strategies have more of a potential to apply sustainable design.

Design with a holistic approach in companies and organizations can unlock capabilities to consider sustainable solutions. This can replace old structures in existing products and services or lead to envisioning new capabilities in the new development process, creating an enormous opportunity to innovate sustainable and prosperous growth to not only produce less harm, but also to ameliorate the social, environmental, and economic conditions.

The results can be astoundingly positive and enriching for the business, the community, consumers and the environment. As stated by Chapman and Gant [13], "Design is a needed, necessary and valuable process of invention and innovation, with the potential to take us closer to a sustainable society."

Designing sustainably requires the ability to think 'upstream.' This means not thinking only of how to reduce the negative impact at the end of the process and the end of the life cycle (setting the filters at the end of the pipelines), but to have the filters in our heads to begin with and design the entire process sustainably. It is easier to control the output this way, rather than trying to fix critical points in a fixed and unsustainable chain.

There are certain strategies to optimize the production and/or consumption structure to make more sustainable interventions. Some sustainable design principles, pointed out by Hans van Weenen [95], which match with the goal of optimizing sustainable consumption will be explained on the following pages.

Waste prevention

- Substitution and reduction
- Change of performance
- Change of the design

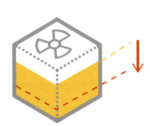

Source reduction

- Reduce the use and generation of insecure substances

Integral chain control

- Awareness of substances and product flow

Eco-cycle society

- Reuse and reclamation
- Efficency of resources
- Waste reduction

WASTE PREVENTION

The concept of waste prevention has a broader focus than exclusively pollution prevention and waste reduction activities primarily from production processes. The prevention of waste generation is defined by J.C. van Weenen as [96]:

"Activities in production, which consist of:
- Substitution and reduction of the use of raw materials;
- Change of the performance of existing products and processes;
- Change of the design of new products and processes.

These activities must result in the non-generation or the reduction of waste and/or its pollution potential, in the materials life cycle."

SOURCE REDUCTION

Source reduction refers to practices that reduce the use or generation of insecure or hazardous substances prior to recycling, treatment or control [37]. The focus of source reduction is clearly on those substances that, due to their quantity, volume or composition, result in problems at the end of their life cycles.

INTEGRAL CHAIN CONTROL

The strategy requires performing an integral life cycle assessment of the environmental impact of a product or service from the initial extraction and processing of raw materials to final disposal or upcycling.
Having integral chain management as a policy principle requires producers and consumers to participate. Both must take into account all the effects on the environment that emerge at any point on the chains of substance flow and look forward and backwards through those chains. Producers and consumers should be aware of the impact of their actions on the environment at any point in the chain, which will help to develop possible improvements and establish the limits of environmental capacity.

An example of this is the realization of cycling processes for substances, materials, components and products to keep a constant flow in those cycles for as long as possible, as well as for the programmed long life of products, as this flow promotes and facilitates the dematerialization process.

The United Nations Environmental Program [93] defines dematerialization as "[…] decreasing the material requirements of whole economies. It requires (a) reducing the material intensity of products and services, i.e., by increasing material efficiency, and (b) especially reducing the use of primary material resources (such as ores, coal, minerals, metals, etc.) by improving recycling and the reuse of secondary materials (i.e., shifting to a circular economy)."

ECO-CYCLE SOCIETY

An eco-cycle society is intended to establish the cyclic management of goods and production, with an emphasis on reuse and reclamation. It aims to realize the most efficient use of resources and to reduce the amount of waste produced at the consumer level in the moment of use, in contrast to the other two strategies, which focus on the production phase.

A circular economy has been implemented in many countries and aims to maximize the use of products that are produced from renewable resources. The goal is to reduce resource input and waste, emission, and energy leakage by minimizing, slowing, closing and narrowing material and energy loops.

Following the same principle, William McDonough [52], in his book *Cradle to Cradle*, indicates that there are two types of metabolism on the planet. There is the biological metabolism (biosphere), which are the cycles of nature, and the technical metabolism (technosphere), namely the cycles of industry.

McDonough and the 'cradle to cradle' approach suggest that the industry must produce goods in a way that all products and materials should be biodegradable and become food for biological cycles, or they should be made of technical materials that remain in closed-loop technical cycles where they continually circulate as valuable nutrients for the industry.

Narodoslawsky, M. [56] had a similar opinion that non-durable products should be based on renewable resources. He points out that resources that pass through the so-called 'bio-cycle' (in which resources are built from substances of the biosphere) serve for short-life products. In contrast, materials originating from non-renewable resources should be fed into the 'mineral cycle' and be used for durable products.

The principal streams for this are technical construction flows and reuse flows. Mineral substances must be used for as long as possible.

In other words, these two principles suggest that non-reusable sources should be used for long-life design products and should not end as waste in a short period of time. At the end of the use phase, they should return to technical cycles by recycling or upcycling the material.

On the contrary, short-life products should be made from renewable resources and returned to biological cycles at the end of the use phase as food or nutrients.

Additionally, Tang and Bhamra [81,4] examined literature that provides an understanding of the psychological and behavioral factors of behavioral change. They identified strategies of Design for Sustainable Behavior (DfSB) that can be applied within a design context to influence user behavior in the direction of a reduction of negative social or environmental use impacts.

The strategies, extracted from the work of Bhamra et al. [5], explain their aim, indicate how they work, and illustrate with examples where they have been applied.

The design interventions are classified by the degree of power in decision-making between the user and the product or service. The seven design approaches fall into three levels of interventions. On the one side is when the power of decision-making lies completely on the user, so the intervention aims to guide the change. The other side is where the power in decision-making derives solely from the intervention and the change must be forced.
This variety of strategies either guide, maintain or ensure the change towards sustainable consumer behavior.

ECO- INFORMATION- EDUCATION

This strategy aims to make consumables visible, understandable and accessible to inspire consumers to reflect upon their use of resources. It works by making the product express the presence and consumption of resources, e.g., water, energy, etc. At the same time, the product encourages the consumer to interact with the resources being used.

Power Aware Cord (Interactive Institute, 2004)
The Power-Aware Cord embeds wires around a cable that pulse light in relation to how much electricity is being drawn on the grid. The more current there is, the blue light spirals brighter and faster. Making the invisible visible tuned consumers in to their bad habits, nudging them to power down and offering some surprising appliance insights: when a radio broadcasts drumbeats and bass riffs, its electricity consumption jumps.

GUIDE
THE CHANGE

provides tangible aural, visual, or tactile signs as reminders to inform users of resource use

Eco- Information

Eco- Choice

Eco- Feedback

MAINTAIN
THE CHANGE

encourages users to behave in ways prescribed by the designer through the embedded affordances and constraints

Eco- Spur

Eco- Steer

ENSURE
THE CHANGE

uses persuasive methods to change what people think or do, sometimes without their knowledge or consent

Eco- Technical

Clever Design

User

Product

Power decision- making

ECO-CHOICE – EMPOWERMENT

With this strategy, consumers are given options to encourage them to think about their behavior and take responsibility for their actions. This works by users having a choice and the product enabling sustainable use to occur.

Efergy eGO Wi-Fi Socket

This appliance is a socket that uses an app to program appliances remotely (turn on and off). The device eliminates the stand-by power of your appliances, and helps to save energy and, consequently, money.

ECO-FEEDBACK – LINKS TO ENVIRONMENTALLY OR SOCIALLY RESPONSIBLE ACTION

Eco-feedback strategies inform users about what they are doing and encourage consumers to make environmentally and socially responsible decisions by offering real-time feedback.
The success of the strategy is that the product provides tangible aural, visual or tactile signs as reminders to inform users of resource use.

Wattson energy monitor

It measures in real time the amount of electricity being used and generated at home or at the office. It shows the values on an easy-to-read display in both numbers and colors. It is comple-mented by Wattson Anywhere, the online portal to access the usage and generation data from any Internet-enabled device.
For users with renewable energy, it is particularly interesting to see how much of the generated electricity is used at home and to monitor the performance of the renewable system.

ECO-SPUR – REWARDS AND PENALTIES INCENTIVES

The strategy is to inspire users to explore more sustainable usage by providing rewards to prompt good behavior or penalties to 'punish' unsustainable usage. The product should show the user the consequences of their actions through 'rewarding incentives' and 'penalties.'

> ## GreenApes- sustainable lifestyle app
> GreenApes is a digital platform for sustainability engagement. It engages people (citizens, customers, employees) in sustainable lifestyles via social networking and gamification. It gives real-life rewards (discount bonus, free gifts, etc.) to users when they perform sustainable actions.

ECO-STEER – AFFORDANCES AND CONSTRAINTS

This facilitates users to adopt more environmentally or socially desirable use habits through the prescriptions and/or constraints of use embedded in the design of the intervention.
This means that the intervention contains affordances and constraints that encourage users to adopt more sustainable use habits or reform their existing unsustainable habits.

> ## Ecover -bio laundry tablets
> The tablets provided can counteract excessive amounts of washing powder consumption by prescribing the correct dose.

ECO-TECHNICAL INTERVENTION

With the combination of design and advanced technology, the aim is to restrain existing use habits and to persuade or control user behavior automatically. The intervention utilizes advanced technology to persuade or control user behavior automatically.

Energy Curtain–Interacting with Daily Light Cycles
During the day, the shade can be drawn to the extent that people choose to collect sunlight and, during the evening, the collected energy is expressed as a glowing pattern on the inside of the shade.

CLEVER DESIGN

Through purely innovative product design, some consumers automatically act environmentally or socially conscious without raising awareness or changing their behavior. The design solution decreases the environmental impact without changing the user's behavior.

Orbital Systems-Purifying and recycling shower
This is an integrated shower system that purifies and recycles the water by Space Certified Technology, enabling up to 90% savings of water and energy. During every shower, it uses the same water in a loop.

SCALES

SCALES is an integrative set of design principles developed by the DEEDS project [8] (Design EDucation and Sustainability) funded by the European Union's Leonardo da Vinci Programme in 2006-2008. It helps designers meet the challenge of designing for sustainability, working at the interface between sustainable production and consumption. It promotes a change of the trajectory of production and consumption patterns.

The principles were published on the DEEDS website, www.deedsproject.org. In 2009, an early overview was published in the International Journal of Innovation and Sustainable Development.

SCALES is a set of 24 mutually complementary principles related to design for sustainability and design for the environment that set comprehensive criteria in different themes:

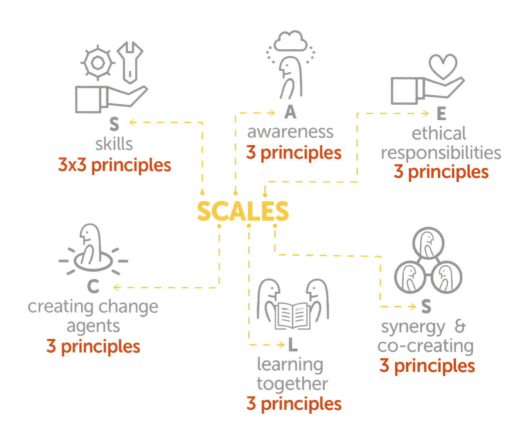

S skills **3x3 principles**

A awareness **3 principles**

E ethical responsibilities **3 principles**

SCALES

C creating change agents **3 principles**

L learning together **3 principles**

S synergy & co-creating **3 principles**

Special Skills

Holistic approach

- S1 – Develop new skills for recognizing, framing (looking for systemic connections) and solving problems.
- S2 – Define problems holistically by systems and Life Cycle Thinking (LCT), combined with appropriate technical and social innovation.
- S3 – Analyze problems from multiple perspectives, including the four sustainability dimensions – economic, human/social, societal/institutional, and environmental – including the full richness of the human dimension (mental, physical, emotional and spiritual).

Eco-efficient production and resource usage

- S4 – Develop Life Cycle Thinking (LCT), and Life Cycle Assessment (LCA) and 'cradle to cradle' skills, be familiar with technology know-how and the appropriate application of lightweighting (materials reduction), renewables/new materials, extended product lives, reusability and recyclability (designing 'quality waste'), waste avoidance, energy issues and dematerialization (moving from products to dematerialized services).
- S5 – Integrate efficient service provision by designing product-service systems (PSS), products suitable for sharing and pooling, pay-per-use or pay-per-experience options.
- S6 – Maximize consumer satisfaction per service enjoyed by addressing human needs: consider different material and immaterial options to do this and choose the most sustainable one; design fertile products offering users an experience, emotion, relation, pride, self-esteem and awareness.

Communication and leadership

- S7 – Lead the agenda - develop leadership skills.
- S8 – Tell engaging stories - develop presentation, narrative, and scenario-setting skills.
- S9 – Forge new versions of enterprise - understand economic thinking without adopting it (know the language, but don't adopt the mindset of business).

Creating change agents

- C1 – Expand your context - be aware that the sustainability context expands the design context in both thinking and practice.
- C2 – Change perceptions - by making use of the diversity of 'value-added' outcomes of DfS.
- C3 – Set new aspirations - practice DfS approaches that provide significant, immediate and visible benefits to encourage consumers to aspire to a new and sustainable cultural representation of the 'good life'.

Awareness

Systemic and context

- A1 – Be aware of context and connections (people, planet, prosperity: key drivers and timeframes).

- A2 – Be aware of positive and negative impacts, feedback loops and side effects in this context.
- A3 – Be aware of choice and responsibility under these circumstances.

Learning together
- L1 – Seek to work with other disciplines; practice inter- and transdisciplinary thinking and practices.
- L2 – Be a teacher-learner; practice mutual learning, creativity and team working to understand sharing ideas as a way to stimulate creativity.
- L3 – Participate with your peers; practice teaching and learning through participation, involving an extended peer community of relevant stakeholders.

Ethical responsibilities
- E1 – Develop designs that do no harm (responsible design, with integrity), but contribute to a sustainable approach to a 'good life', over the long term and globally, and also if applied in mass production.
- E2 – Create genuine consumer empowerment; offer designs that enhance personal standing and acceptance, and thus social sustainability, and encourage user involvement (consumer empowerment).
- E3 – Focus on experiences, not objects; develop practical, functional, and fun designs that deepen life experiences and strengthen personal and social cohesion.

Synergy and co-creating
- S1 – Activate through participation; promote the development of teams, communities and networks.
- S2 – Engage in synergistic clusters of competence.
- S3 – Practice collaboration, sharing and partnering, and involve stakeholders in the problem definition and solution design process.

ECO-EFFICIENCY AND ECO-EFFECTIVENESS OF PRODUCTION AND CONSUMPTION

It is not a hidden truth that for the industry, in the economic dimension of production, profitability is the main motive that drives the production system, rather than the desire to satisfy human needs. Nonetheless, production innovation is the most understood and widely used strategy for a transition towards sustainability. Moreover, other stages of the chain must be evaluated for a broader, more sustainable transition.

Eco-efficiency and eco-effectiveness are metrics that consider aspects (efficiency, effectiveness, durability and the convenient fulfillment of functional and symbolic needs and wants) of the whole production and consumption chain translated into the satisfaction of users at minimum costs and with the lowest negative impact.

On the one hand, eco-efficiency is the improved environmental performance of a product through the selection of low-impact materials, the reduction of material usage, reduced energy consumption, and reduced waste and pollution per functional unit of a product during its life cycle [77, 52].

Applied to consumption, eco-efficiency can be defined as the ratio between consumer satisfaction and the activated resources to achieve it. The goal is to maximize satisfaction with the lowest possible use of resources.

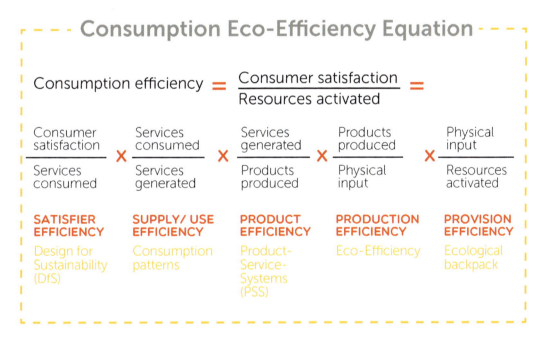

Graphic based on Spangenberg. J.H.

On the other hand, eco-effectiveness means improving the total impact on the environment when consumer needs are satisfied not only by the function in question, but also by additional fulfillments around it.

The concept of eco-effectiveness proposes the transformation of products and their associated material flows, such that they form a supportive relationship with ecological systems and future economic growth. The goal is not to minimize the cradle to grave flow of materials, but to generate cyclical, cradle to cradle metabolisms that enable materials to maintain their status as resources over time (upcycling).

Consequently, <u>eco-effectiveness may be seen as doing the right thing in long-term planning. Eco-efficiency may instead be understood as doing things right in a short-term performance.</u> Therefore, it is indeed necessary to address these long- and short-term assessments simultaneously.

Fluorescent lamps.
Eco-effectiveness VS. Eco-efficiency

An example of the difference between eco-effectiveness and eco-efficiency and the crucial correlation between them are fluorescent lighting systems. They spread rapidly during World War II, and by 1951, more light was produced in the United States by fluorescent lamps than by incandescent lamps. Fluorescent bulbs were supposed to be the invention of the century, as they are more energy-efficient and burn less energy in comparison to conventional light bulbs. However, these compact fluorescent light bulbs contain mercury, which is highly toxic and particularly harmful to the brain of both fetuses and children. This aspect is highly problematic, especially when a bulb breaks. With the fluorescent light bulb, one problem was solved, but another was created. The solution is energy-efficient, but the bulbs are made from toxic substances. It is far from being an effective solution to clean power.

Another more recent case in the mobility sector is the emerging car-sharing business model in Germany. On average, a privately owned car is used less than 60 minutes per day, representing 4% of the time, while the other 96% of the time it is parked [65]. This leads to an accumulated use time of less than six months over 12 years of the product's life. Seen this way, to own and drive a car is not very eco-efficient and it is easy to detect possibilities for improvement in the use phase socio-culturally, rather than technically. For instance, there can be an improvement of the use intensity by sharing instead of owning.

This was proven in the case of DriveNow. The floating car-sharing service improves city mobility and increases the promotion of local mobility in urban areas. Cars are picked up and dropped off anywhere in the city. The service is a joint venture between BMW and the car rental company Sixt. According to BMW's company surveys [67], 38% of DriveNow customers have sold a personal vehicle as a result of using the car-sharing service. It sounds like a highly efficient service, but in the entire life cycle of the service and products involved, it fails to develop aspects that are both eco-effective and eco-efficient. For instance, when it comes to the type of energy used by the cars, all of them should be electric, not petroleum fuel or diesel cars. Similarly, it can be questioned whether the cars are developed, designed and built in a way that the materials and parts can return to a technical cycle and be disassembled, dismantled, recycled and upcycled or to a biological cycle and be compostable.

However, the shift of car-use behavior achieved by DriveNow is part of a recent global trend. Today's shift from ownership to access is a visible trend that is gaining power every day and will be a major economic driver in the future. It changes the medieval paradigm of the relation between the terms wealth and ownership. One of the principles of a circular economy is to offer products as services, instead of conventionally selling products. The products are taken by the customers and they pay for the time or usage, for either a short or long contract period, like the case of DriveNow and many other shared mobility services.

*Eco-effectiveness
may be seen as doing
the right thing in
long-term planning.
Eco-efficiency
may instead be
understood as
doing things right
in a short-term
performance.*

This section has introduced a range of different concepts, definitions and strate-gies that can be used to support design for sustainable consumption in the different stages of the product or service development process. These are just a few of the many ideas that can be found in literature. Through a quick web search, one can find many more. However, I consider the selection presented in this book to be especially relevant to designers. The combination of information, inspiration, education, exem-plification and guidance makes designers more involved and committed to a sus-tainable future and enables them to contribute by designing products and services to change consumer behavior and promote sustainable production and consumption.

Both consumer behavior change strategies and sustainable design strategies, like the nudging techniques and the behavior wizard, as well as the scales and sustain-able design principles, and design interventions should be implemented to reach a sustainable level in the interventions. These sustainable consumption and produc-tion strategies, applied to increase innovation, use low-impact materials, optimize processes and manufacturing, make distribution more efficient, reduce the impact of use and optimize the life cycle, should aim to make consumers have more sustain-able consumption habits.

The strategies presented above can be combined and used on a mix-and-match basis. The next section presents the tool that I developed based on these strategies and concepts to make a roadmap to help designers apply them in the design process from start to finish.

ROADMAP

*Sustainable consumer behavior
+ Sustainable design strategies + User types
+ Service and product design*

This section describes my proposed tool in detail. The roadmap assists designers in the design process to produce sustainable and innovative solutions to change consumer behavior towards a more sustainable lifestyle and consumption.

The tool combines best practices, theories, concepts and strategies from the BASICS section. The integration of the framework from different disciplines (consumer behavior, service design, sustainable design, psychology and design for behavior change) gives a holistic and complete approach to apply in the design process. The contribution and relevance of the tool is the merging of various elements in a sustainable consumer-centric way to enhance the probability of having more sustainable outcomes.

This tool should be used as a systemic guidance map or toolbox to <u>place sustainability at the center of the design process from idea generation, through implementation, up to the creation of new solutions for complex consumption-related challenges</u>. However, it is not a rigorous step-by-step manual detailing how a design project should be conducted.

The roadmap consist of six stages: 1) defining the desired behavior and target consumer type, 2) understanding the psychology of consumers, 3) selecting the most suitable design intervention type, 4) choosing the facilitator strategies to take action implicit in the intervention, 5) generating the idea and concept (compilation of design properties) and finally 6) evaluating or assessing the process to learn and improve.

The stages can be used and combined in almost any way, meaning that there is not just one way of using the roadmap. Indeed, experimenting with new combinations and altering the order might be a better solution for some projects in which including as many sustainable touch points as possible is needed.

The success of designing a more sustainable intervention that changes consumer behavior involves finding the right combination between conceptualizing, developing, prototyping and evaluating ideas through a continuous process of gradual improvements.

DEFINE BEHAVIOR

DEFINE
TARGET USER/
CONSUMER

DESIGNING SUSTAINABLE
CONSUMER BEHAVIOR
ROAD MAP
6 STEPS

TYPE OF DESIGN
INTERVENTION

FACILITATOR
STRATEGIES TO
TAKE ACTION

CONCEPT /
DESIGN PROPERTIES

EVALUATION

DESIGNING SUSTAINABLE
CONSUMPTION ROADMAP

Project

DEFINE DESIRED BEHAVIOR

How is it now?
Actual negative impact
Behavior name
Description

Why is it not being changed?

Type of desired behavior

PERMANENT
SPECIFIC TIME
ONE TIME

New behavior
Familiar
Increase
Decrease
Stop

DEFINE TARGET USER/ CONSUMER

Who & how are the most frequent users
External factors

Internal factors: (attitudes, habits, life events, routines)
Contextual trends, social or personal capabilities

Enthusiastic   Undecided   Worried   Irresponsible

TYPE OF DESIGN INTERVENTION

Guide the change

Eco-Information
Eco-Choice
Eco-Feedback

Mantain the change

Eco-Spur
Eco-Steer

Ensure the change

Eco-Technical
Clever design

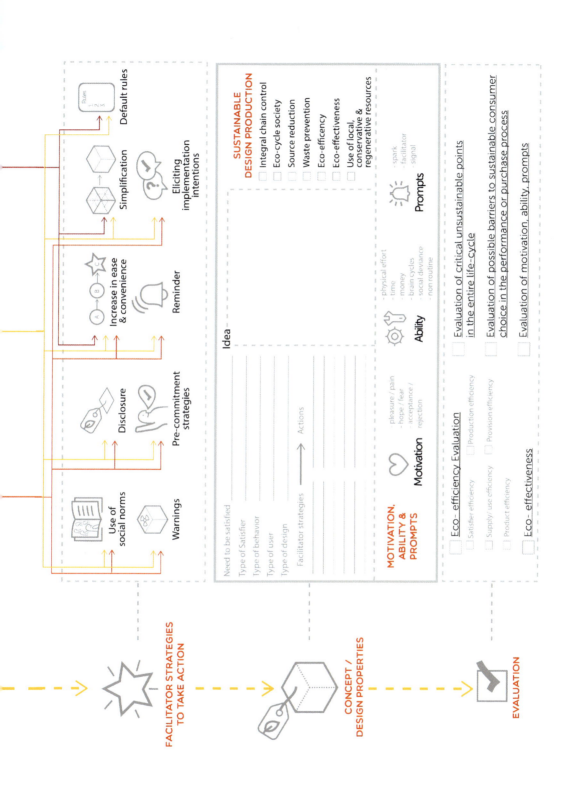

FACILITATOR STRATEGIES
TO TAKE ACTION

Use of social norms

Warnings

Disclosure

Pre-commitment strategies

Increase in ease & convenience

Reminder

Simplification

Eliciting implementation intentions

Default rules

Rules
1
2
3

CONCEPT /
DESIGN PROPERTIES

Idea

Need to be satisfied
Type of Satisfier
Type of behavior
Type of user
Type of design

Facilitator strategies → Actions

MOTIVATION, ABILITY & PROMPTS

Motivation
- pleasure / pain
- hope / fear
- acceptance / rejection

Ability
- physical effort
- time
- money
- brain cycles
- social deviance
- non routine

Prompts
- spark
- facilitator
- signal

SUSTAINABLE
DESIGN PRODUCTION

☐ Integral chain control
☐ Eco-cycle society
☐ Source reduction
☐ Waste prevention
☐ Eco-efficency
☐ Eco-effectiveness
☐ Use of local, conservative & regenerative resources

EVALUATION

Eco-efficiency Evaluation
☐ Satisfier efficiency   ☐ Production efficiency
☐ Supply use efficiency   ☐ Provision efficiency
☐ Product efficiency

Eco-effectiveness

☐ Evaluation of critical unsustainable points in the entire life-cycle

☐ Evaluation of possible barriers to sustainable consumer choice in the performance or purchase process

☐ Evaluation of motivation, ability, prompts

DEFINE DESIRED BEHAVIOR

ROADMAP

DEFINE DESIRED BEHAVIOR

How is it now? _____

Actual negative impact _____

Behavior name _____

Description _____

_____

Why is it not being changed? _____

Type of desired behavior

PERMANENT

SPECIFIC TIME

ONE TIME

New behavior
Familiar
Increase
Decrease
Stop

In the first stage—in some cases, after receiving the design brief—designers must determine their goal in terms of the behavior that they are aiming to achieve.
It is recommended to start thinking about how the situation is right now, what unsustainable behavior is aimed to be changed, who is performing it and how, and what negative impact there is on the environment.
One example of the definition of a desired behavior is the consumption pattern of plastics when shopping for daily groceries in supermarkets. The current behavior is to overuse plastic, generating large amounts of waste due to excess packaging and the use of plastic bags. The new desired behavior would be to reduce the amount of plastic used during the entire process of shopping at the supermarket.

In this step, designers must describe and synthesize the desired behavior as specifically, clearly and in as much detail as possible. This information will help to define the type of behavior aimed for that, pursuant to Fogg´s behavior grid, could be classified in one of the 15 possible behaviors according to the purpose and duration of the behavior.

Following the previous example, in most regular supermarkets, there is a strong tendency to over package products and give away or sell plastic bags to carry the groceries home. The negative impact is that most of these plastic bags are used one time and then disposed of, contributing to the large amount of household waste produced. The targeted behavior to change this situation and modify consumer habits when shopping will make them prefer products with less packaging and encourage them to carry the groceries home using other alternatives.

In most cases, this behavior is not performed for two main reasons: 1) supermarkets do not provide more sustainable alternatives and 2) consumers often shop spontaneously, so they do not seek out stores with eco-friendly products in advance, nor do they bring their own shopping bags. Following the tool, in this case, the targeted behavior is to change consumers permanently (to use fewer plastic bags and choose products with less packaging) in performing a familiar action (when buying groceries at the supermarket, to bring their own bags).
The strategies to tackle the 15 different types of behavior will be amplified in step number five 'Concept/design properties.'

DEFINE TARGET USER/ CONSUMERS

ROADMAP

DEFINE
TARGET USER/
CONSUMER

Who & how are the _____
most frequent users _____

External factors _____

Internal factors: (attitudes,
habits, life events, routines) _____

Contextual trends, social
or personal capabilities _____

Enthusiastic   Undecided   Worried   Irresponsible

Identifying the target user/consumer (also known in marketing and design as the target market) helps designers develop effective strategies. A target market is a set of individuals sharing similar needs or characteristics intended to perform the desired behavior by using or consuming the service or product. Designers need to know exactly (or as exactly as possible) who those individuals are.
Geographic, demographic and psychographic data are the three main ways to find the target market.

One of the biggest mistakes is trying to reach everyone. <u>Strategies must be tailored to match the different orientations, values, goals, lifestyles, attitudes and social backgrounds of people in order to appeal to them and satisfy their particular needs.</u>
Likewise, in any design process, the target market (in this case, the consumers that will perform the behavior) can start being defined by identifying the following demographic factors:

- Age
- Location
- Gender
- Income level
- Education level
- Marital or family status
- Occupation
- Ethnic background

One must also consider the psychographics, which means the more personal characteristics of a person, including:

- Personality
- Attitudes
- Values
- Interests/hobbies
- Lifestyles
- Behavior

At this stage, data collection can be done through survey questionnaires or tools, such as cluster or association analysis. This process would result in statistically significant, but not detailed, information. Thus, it is important to conduct further research, preferably with qualitative methods, such as laddering interviews, focus groups, etc. With these methods, it is possible to have detailed user types that explain users' beliefs, their past and current behaviors and experiences in relation to the type of behavior that designers are trying to encourage (the selected desired behavior).

The second step in the definition of the target market is to classify the target user/consumer into four different types based on their sustainable attitude and intentions: Enthusiastic, Worried, Undecided or Irresponsible. This will help the designer select the right design type and the most suitable strategies to reach consumers and encourage them to perform a sustainable behavior.
It is possible in a project to have more than just one type of user, i.e., regular consumers of organic food products can be both enthusiastic and worried.

In that case, it is important to point out an estimated percentage of each type to prioritize the strategies to: a) reach the largest group or b) simultaneously apply different strategies to reach both types equally. However, in the first option (reaching the larger group), additional facilitators that work for the smaller group type can be implemented in the strategy to reach them at a lower scale.

Strategies must be tailored to match the different orientations, values, goals, lifestyles, attitudes and social backgrounds of people in order to appeal to them and satisfy their particular needs.

TYPE OF DESIGN INTERVENTION

ROADMAP

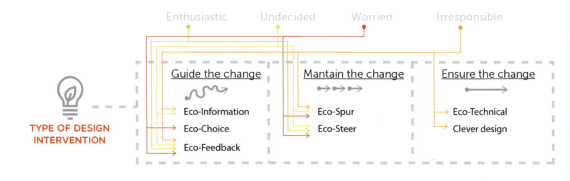

This stage involves selecting the appropriate design strategy based on the detailed consumer types created in the previous stage.

Design strategies are matched with the consumer types by using psychological variables to reach the best strategy for the intervention.
Each of the four types has different hypothetical pro-environmental interventions that match better to ensure a more suitable sustainable solution for their needs, attitudes and intentions. However, when designing, if the target group includes more than one consumer type, it's practical to choose design strategies that are effective for multiple types.
The strategies, besides being classified by the degree of power of decision-making between the user and product, can also be classified in three categories: instructional, motivational or supportive.

	Enthusiastic	Irresponsible	Worried	Undecided
Intention	ALREADY DOING	NO	YES	NO
Type of design intervention	Eco-Feedback Eco-Steer	Eco-Feedback Eco-Spur Eco-Information Clever design, Eco-Technology	Eco-Choice Eco-Feedback Eco-Steer Eco-Spur	Eco-Information Eco-Feedback Eco-Steer Eco-Spur
	Supportive	Instructional, motivational & supportive	Motivational & supportive	Instructional & motivational

Enthusiastic consumers: The performance of pro-environmental behaviors in enthusiastic consumers may not be constant due to the lack or disappearance of motivation or the emergence of new barriers.

For this reason, enthusiastic users need supportive strategies to make the desired behavior a habit and maintain it over time.

Communication towards them should focus on the rightness of their behavior. Markets or policy makers could cheer their efforts and emphasize all the benefits associated with sustainable consumption, both for themselves as individual consumers and for the broader environment and society.

Irresponsible consumers: These users tend to ignore environmental topics and do not feel responsible for environmental problems. Changing the mindset of this group would be the best tactic, but also the most challenging one.

A more feasible short-term strategy is to enhance involvement by stressing the personal benefits of sustainable consumption with a focus on 'selfish' needs. Individualistic needs, such as security concerns, health consequences, hedonistic needs and the need for economic reasoning could be used to stimulate the consumption of sustainable products and services. Step by step, the awareness can be created to achieve the greater goal of mindset changing.

Designers need to consider all three types of intervention strategies—motivational, instructive and supportive—in order to make these consumers aware of environmental issues. The design must make pro-environmental behaviors desirable for consumers by targeting their motivation.

Information, eco-feedback and rewards are ideal for the long-term goal of changing their mindset, but intelligent products that act sustainably on behalf of the consumer are best to motivate and make them act sustainably in the short term.

Worried consumers: They do not have the intention of performing pro-environmental actions due to their routine-oriented lifestyle. They are not very open to changing their routines. Support and motivation to act might increase their self-confidence and consequently lead to action. Worried users can be encouraged by both supportive and motivational strategies, such as behavior steering, rewards and competition.

Undecided consumers: Even though they are concerned about the ways to decrease their negative impact on the environment, they are reluctant to act due to insufficient knowledge or behavioral control. A potentially successful strategy is to underline and confirm the social norms and apply pressure from peers to whom these consumers are subject.

This type of user can be motivated by instructional and motivational intervention strategies, such as normative feedback, rewards and eco-feedback.

As a general conclusion, the strategies that guide change have a better response with consumers that have a positive attitude and intention towards sustainable consumption. However, these interventions are a great complement to supporting the transition of changing less responsible consumers into enthusiastic or worried consumers. The strategies to maintain the change nudge consumers to act, and are therefore suggested for those with a tendency towards the behavior-intention gap.
These strategies can bridge, in a smoother and easier way, the decision-making process (particularly of undecided and worried consumers) towards the choosing of more sustainable alternatives. Both eco-spur and eco-steer interfere with automatic thinking and make consumers reflect on their actions following an easier and more convenient path when the disruption occurs (do something to get a reward, skip a penalty or due to affordances or constraints).

On the contrary, interventions that force the change work perfectly for all types of consumers because, without much awareness, the behavior is changed automatically by making the intervention act sustainably on behalf of the consumer. Therefore, they force a behavior on irresponsible consumers who tend to refuse conscious changes.

Each of the four types has different hypothetical pro-environmental interventions that match better to ensure a more suitable sustainable solution for their needs, attitudes and intentions.

FACILITATOR STRATEGIES TO TAKE ACTION

ROADMAP

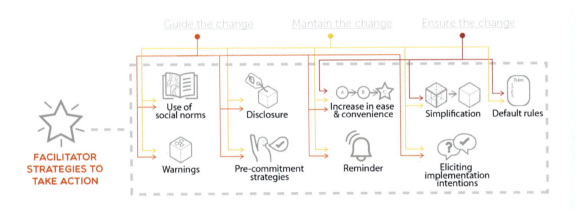

MAKE THEM BEHAVE SUSTAINABLY

Facilitator strategies help to take action by using nudging techniques. The understanding of nudges as elements of the designed environment will ensure the influence on people to behave in particular ways, without constraining their freedom.

As mentioned earlier, how these techniques should be applied to the interventions depends on the circumstances and goals of the desired behavior.
The facilitator strategies are matched with the three types of design intervention, according to the intention of each of them. For instance, the 'guide for change' interventions require much more information to be offered and they need to have direct contact with the consumer to get their attention, increase awareness, change their perception and intention, and consequently achieve the performance of the desired behavior.

However, the facilitators can be applied to all types of interventions. There is no one-to-one correspondence between design interventions and nudge facilitator strategies. An intervention may require different facilitators, or contrarily, it might require only one for the behavior to be performed. Nonetheless, the more facilitators are used, the higher the chances are that users will be nudged at different levels to perform the desired behavior.

CONCEPT / DESIGN PROPERTIES

ROADMAP

CONCEPT /
DESIGN PROPERTIES

Need to be satisfied _____ Idea
Type of satisfier _____
Type of behavior _____
Type of user _____
Type of design _____

Facilitator strategies ⟶ Actions
_____
_____
_____
_____

SUSTAINABLE
DESIGN
PRODUCTION
☐ Integral chain control
☐ Eco-cycle society
☐ Source reduction
☐ Waste prevention
☐ Eco-efficency
☐ Eco- effectiveness
☐ Use of local,
  conservative &
  regenerative resources

MOTIVATION,
ABILITY &
PROMPTS

Motivation
- pleasure / pain
- hope / fear
- acceptance /
  rejection

Ability
- physical effort
- time
- money
- brain cycles
- social deviance
- non routine

Prompts
- spark
- facilitator
- signal

In this stage, the design team should gather information and co-work with as many people involved as possible, including designers, test users, usability engineers and all other stakeholders. The co-working process aims to generate the concept and idea of the product or service to make it more feasible from different perspectives to ensure that it will help users perform the sustainable behavior.

Likewise, as in every design process, during the ideation and concept stage, designers spark new ideas in the form of questions and solutions. Free-thinking, creative and curious activities are highly welcomed. In the stage of idea generation, the aim is to produce a large quantity of ideas that potentially inspire newer, better and more sustainable solutions. Afterwards, the team can filter and narrow them down into the best, most practical and most sustainable ones.

It is important to emphasize that this stage of ideation, concept and configuration of design properties is a process that might take several months until there is a concrete result that can be produced, which is normal in the product or service design process.

On the first section in this stage of the map (when possible), it is recommended to determine the need to be satisfied and the type of satisfier that the intervention will be. This will help to remember the goal and simultaneously broaden the spectrum of possible solutions without being enclosed in a single predetermined solution. The selected aspects of the previous stages should be compiled and summarized to have a better overview of the reason why, to whom, when, and the what of the intervention, enabling one to craft a meaningful and actionable problem statement. This should be a guide that focuses on insights and needs with the particular characteristics selected.

The second stage of this step is to shape the idea and turn it into solutions combining the understanding of the problem, the consumers for whom the intervention is designed, and the sustainable aspects to be integrated in the intervention.

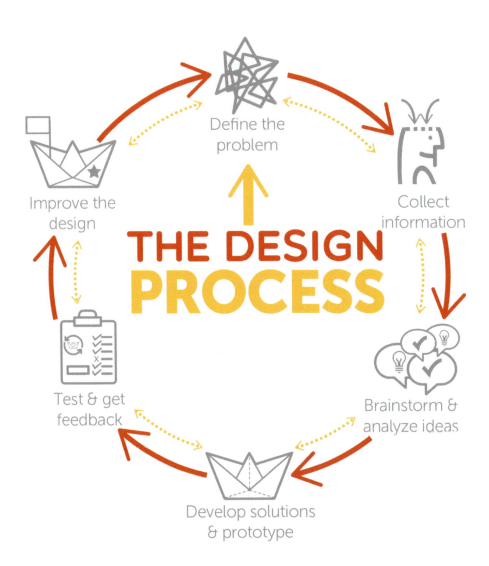

THE DESIGN
PROCESS

Define the
problem

Collect
information

Brainstorm &
analyze ideas

Develop solutions
& prototype

Test & get
feedback

Improve the
design

MAKE THEM BEHAVE SUSTAINABLY

Sustainable design strategies stage

The sustainable design strategies stage is the most important part of the map because these strategies ensure that the output of the intervention will be sustainable by reducing carbon emissions, as well as toxic and hazardous substances, to reduce consumers' ecological footprint. The strategies must be applied throughout the entire design process using an integrated approach to create 'win-win-win' solutions—for the environment, for the consumer and for the company.

The main objectives of the sustainable design strategies are to reduce or completely avoid the critical use of resources like energy, water and raw materials, as well as prevent environmental degradation caused by pollutants, hazardous materials and waste used throughout the product life cycle.

Designers need to focus on achieving the requirements of these sustainable design strategies in all the different stages of the life cycle of the product or service in order to ensure a sustainable product from its production and use to its disposal or upcycling.

Waste Prevention
- Substitution and reduction of raw materials used both in the production and in the use of the product.
- Change of the performance of existing products, processes and services to make them more sustainable through the entire life cycle.
- Change of the design of new products and processes is key to ensuring new sustainable goods.

Source Reduction
This involves the implementation of practices that reduce the use or generation of dangerous or hazardous substances prior to recycling, treatment or control that might cause problems during their use and end of their life cycle.
There is a special focus on materials and substances that imply a critical extraction or transformation with major environmental and social impact, such as nuclear waste, chemicals that may be teratogens or carcinogens and petroleum derivatives, among others.

Substances, materials and metals like arsenic, cadmium, chromium, mercury, lead, polyvinyl chloride (PVC), polyvinylidene chloride (PVDC), chlorinated polyvinyl chloride (CPVC), and polychloroprene, among others, should be avoided or even banned in production due to their tendency to accumulate in the biosphere and consequently lead to irreversible negative human health effects, as well as a negative environmental impact.

Integral Chain Control

It is indeed necessary to account for the carbon footprint of the designed intervention, measuring the emissions at each stage of the product's life cycle, including:

- Extraction and production of raw materials
- Transportation of raw materials
- Production (or service provision)
- Distribution
- Product use
- Disposal/recycling/upcycling

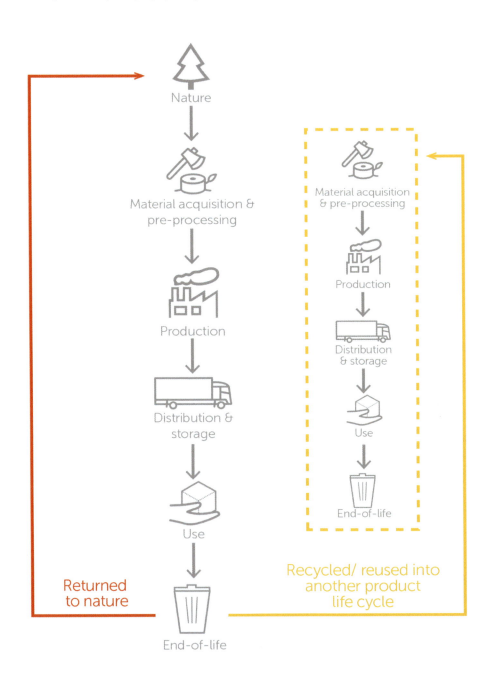

At each stage, the analysis should include greenhouse gas emissions and the use of resources resulting from any material inputs to, or outputs from, the process. Commonly, this includes energy and water use, transportation, fuel, direct gas emissions and waste. In the case of a service product, the life cycle stages are defined individually for each service.

It is recommended for companies to use a process map to successfully understand, assess and improve the life cycle of a product or service. This tool illustrates the processes, materials, and energy needed to move a product through its life cycle. Thus, a broad panorama from start to finish can be displayed to identify the problematic and unsustainable points along the chain.

Once the entire life cycle is visible and clear, it is possible to calculate the environmental impact of an intervention from start to finish. Only in that moment is it possible to evaluate and assess the different alternatives for materials and processes based on real data to choose the best fit for the sustainable values being pursued. However, for the design team, it is sometimes difficult, as well as time- and resource-consuming, to make a detailed and deep life cycle assessment. In the Netherlands, Pré Consultants created the tool Eco-Indicator 99 [64], which allows designers to calculate the environmental impact of a product or design in a simpler and easier way, measuring with standard indicators scores of frequently used materials and processes.

To carry out the analysis, designers must create a detailed list of component parts by disassembling the product and identifying the materials and processes that make up each part. Every element is added to the correct section on the table and quantified in relevant units (for example, raw materials in kilograms, electricity in kilowatt hours, and transport in tons per kilometer).

The next step is to look up the Eco-Indicator value for each element from the tables. The tool provides a list of materials and processes with their own assigned value. The Eco-Indicator value is a representation of the impact of a product, material, or process based on data from the life cycle assessment and its effect on human health, ecosystem quality and resource use. The weight or measure of each element is multiplied by the Eco-Indicator value to give the eco-points. The higher the points, the worse the environmental impact of the element is. The total number of eco-points can be calculated for each life cycle stage of the product or service.

The list of the Eco-Indicator 99 has values available for materials, production processes, transport processes, energy generation processes and disposal scenarios. The tool and all the associated worksheets can be downloaded for free from: www.pre.nl

Simple process map of a Bike

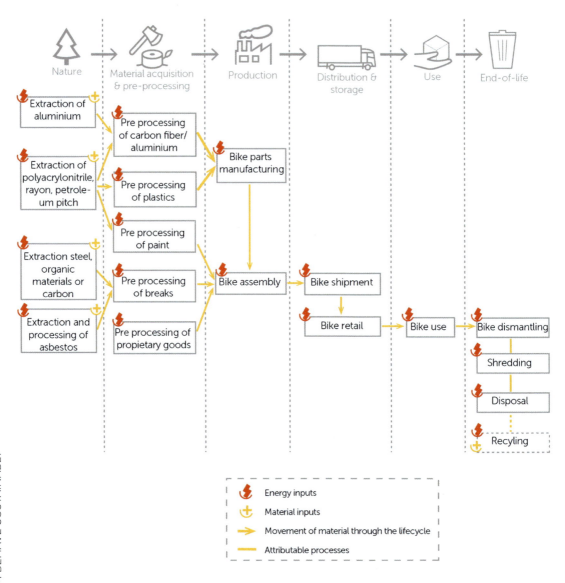

Nature

Material acquisition & pre-processing

Production

Distribution & storage

Use

End-of-life

Extraction of aluminium

Extraction of polyacrylonitrile, rayon, petroleum pitch

Extraction steel, organic materials or carbon

Extraction and processing of asbestos

Pre processing of carbon fiber/ aluminium

Pre processing of plastics

Pre processing of paint

Pre processing of breaks

Pre processing of propietary goods

Bike parts manufacturing

Bike assembly

Bike shipment

Bike retail

Bike use

Bike dismantling

Shredding

Disposal

Recyling

Energy inputs

Material inputs

Movement of material through the lifecycle

Attributable processes

Eco-cycle society

Designers must aim to build a society based on the cyclic management of goods and production, with an emphasis on recycling, reuse and reclamation. This includes the prevention of waste, change patterns of consumption, more efficient production methods and waste management with a greater focus on recycling. Design and material selection, as well as energy consumption in manufacturing and use, must be taken into account. In addition, sustainable cycles can only be achieved if a greater proportion of waste can be compostable as biological nutrients, reused or recycled.

Ability, motivation & prompts section

In this section, designers must understand if users have the motivation and necessary ability to perform the desired behavior. Depending on the type of behavior desired, the best methods must be chosen to intervene in the ability, and motivation of users, as well as to prompt the behavior.

To perform every action, the behavior must be prompted when the person is both motivated and able to perform it. For each of the 15 behavior types, there are different methods for persuading consumers to perform the desired behavior. The methods for each of the behavior types according to Fogg's behavior wizard tool [26] will be explained here. The grid and additional information can be found at: www.behaviorwizard.org

Do a new behavior one time:
Example: Install a low-flow showerhead.
These behaviors are often used at early stages of complex behavior inductions. The main challenge with this type of behavior is the lack of ability. Since it occurs only once, the consumer must have enough knowledge to successfully complete the action on their first attempt. Otherwise, frustration, and quitting, may occur.
To achieve this action, three elements must come together at once. The consumer must be prompted when the person is both motivated and has the ability to perform it. To achieve the behavior, the prompt should be coupled with a motivational or facilitative element. Also, to increase the ability of the subject, it is recommended to explain the new behavior in terms of one that is familiar, as well as to increase the motivation of the consumer by explicitly highlighting the benefits of the new behavior.

Do a new behavior for a period of time:
Example: Buy in bulk to reduce packaging for one month.
In this type of behavior, the prompt is a request to commit on doing something for a fixed period of time. The first challenge is to shape the new behavior in a way that reduces costs in terms of money, effort, time, etc., and at the same time increases benefits. The second challenge is to prompt the action at the optimal moment. To achieve this, it is important to boost motivation while simultaneously downplaying

A PRODUCT'S CARBON FOOTPRINT

CAN HELP TO **DIFFERENTIATE** YOUR PRODUCT OR SERVICE AND ENHANCE YOUR BRAND

factors that de-motivate. It is desirable to increase the ability required to make the commitment and perform the behavior, and deliver the prompt (request to commit) when motivation and ability are both high. These habits tend to fail to reach the target audience. The main reason is that the change is too much too fast. Thus, to achieve this type of behavior, besides breaking it down into simpler habits, it is good to stack them on top of each other one at a time until the whole habit becomes automatic near the end of the established duration.

Do a new behavior permanently:

Example: Decide to always use energy-efficient light bulbs.

These behaviors imply a life change and have two main challenges: commitment (agreeing to the change) and fulfillment (behaving in these new ways). The fulfillment part is much like permanently doing a familiar behavior, because the new behavior will soon become familiar. Thus, it's important to focus on the unique aspect: getting people to commit to a lifelong change. To achieve this, motivation must be boosted (if needed), ability must be enhanced by making the commitment act simple, and the prompt should be issued when motivation and ability are in optimal states.

The challenge is to influence the target audience to perform the behavior and then get them to repeat it from Day One onward. Most new habits are not achieved in one step or one intervention; instead, they require a sequence of behaviors.

Do a familiar behavior one time:

Example: Plant a tree.

These behaviors are among the easiest to achieve because the person is already familiar with the behavior and knows how to perform it. In addition, consumers already have a notion of the costs and benefits when performing it. To achieve this type of behavior, the prompt must tell a person to "do this behavior NOW" on a regular basis during the specified period of time. At the same time, the consumer must have sufficient motivation and ability when the prompt occurs.

With these behaviors, people do not require much reassurance (enhancing motivation) or step-by-step instructions (increasing ability). The biggest challenge is timing: finding a way to deliver an effective prompt at the right moment when the person is already motivated and able.

Do a familiar behavior for a period of time:

Example: Go by bike to work each day during the summer.

To achieve this behavior, a prompt must tell a person to "do this behavior NOW." The person must have sufficient motivation and ability when the prompt occurs. Since success itself in these behaviors is motivating, it is crucial to design the motivation-inducing elements of these behavior strategies into the initial part of the intervention. Over time, as the familiar behavior in a specific period of time is created, people do not require reassurance (enhancing motivation) or step-by-step instructions (increasing ability). Instead, it is necessary to remind the subject to perform the action (to prompt the behavior) throughout the desired duration.

Do a familiar behavior permanently:

Example: Unplug appliances when they are not being used from now on.

All of us have developed many familiar and permanent behaviors in our lives, such as brushing our teeth or checking emails. These behaviors are the most valuable of the 15 behavior types. In commercial terms, any company that can create this behavior in its customers will most likely profit, as these behaviors are not easily broken. However, this behavior requires, in most cases, a sequence of steps, or a route, that people take on their way to achieving them. Sequencing is a key element. If the intervention focuses on a single step, it is likely to fail.

The best examples of these behaviors begin with a simpler goal that starts by convincing the subject to do a new behavior one time.

The challenge with these behaviors is also timing: finding a way to deliver a prompt at a moment when the person is already motivated and able. To ensure the achievement of the action, the prompt must tell a person to "do this behavior NOW" when both motivation and ability are in ideal states to perform the behavior.

Increase a behavior one time:

Example: Buy more vegetables today, rather than meat.

These behaviors can stretch people, and that's often the point. By pushing their limits, people can gain insights and confidence into increasing the performance of acting more sustainably in different areas.

These behaviors play a role in self-improvement processes. To achieve these behaviors, the prompt leading to the desired behavior should be coupled with a motivational element. The ability to perform the behavior must be increased (make it easier to do) and the motivation for doing the behavior can be strengthened with appropriate intrinsic or extrinsic rewards.

Increase a behavior for a period of time:

Example: Eat more local and seasonal fruits and vegetables each day during the summer.

In this type of behavior, the audience knows the behavior; they have already done it before. What is new is doing the behavior more intensely. This may mean with more effort, longer or with more focus. In other words, it is about taking an existing behavior and intensifying it.

These behaviors are intended to have an end point, which means that getting people to commit to them is easier than committing them to do it permanently. Also, their adherence is likely to be better. To achieve the performance of the behavior, the number of prompts leading to the desirable behavior should increase. Simultaneously, the ability to perform the behavior is enhanced (make it easier to do) and the motivation is amplified for doing the behavior with intrinsic and extrinsic motivators.

Increase a behavior permanently:

Example: Increase the use of biodegradable cleaning products and gradually replace your non-eco-friendly ones.

To achieve these behaviors, as with the previous behavior, the number of prompts leading to the desirable behavior should increase. This goes along with enhancing the ability to perform the behavior (make it easier to do) and amplifying the motivation for doing the behavior with intrinsic and extrinsic motivators.

Decrease a behavior one time:
Example: Take a shorter shower today.

These behaviors are often an early step towards permanent behavior change. For example, spending less energy in one month can help people learn how to save energy in their houses and reduce their energy consumption in the future. As you might expect, people are more successful in achieving these behaviors than making the permanent change. Creating success by decreasing one-time behaviors has been shown to matter in achieving a behavior of a longer duration. In other words, a small step can lead to a more enduring behavior change.

To achieve the performance, removing the prompt that leads to the undesirable behavior is the first step. Also, the ability to perform the behavior must be reduced (make it harder to do) and the motivation for doing the behavior should be replaced with de-motivators: pain, fear or social rejection.

Decrease a behavior for a period of time:
Example: Use less energy for air conditioning during the summer.

These behaviors are common in interventions for health (eat less), environment (consume less), and personal financial security (spend less). A reduction program for a fixed period helps people to see how a long-term change might be possible. In other words, they can represent a step towards a permanent decrease.

To remove the prompt that leads to the undesirable behavior, reduce the ability to perform the behavior (make it harder to do) and replace the motivation for doing the behavior with de-motivators: pain, fear or social rejection can help to achieve the performance of the positive behavior.

Decrease a behavior permanently:
Example: Buy less 'fast fashion' clothing from now on.

In a typical case, the behavior being reduced is not desirable, but stopping the behavior completely may not be practical or possible. That is when permanently decreasing the behavior is the appropriate target behavior.

As in the other decreasing behaviors, the strategies to achieve it are to remove the prompt that leads to the undesirable behavior, reduce the ability to perform the behavior (make it harder to do) and replace the motivation for doing the behavior with de-motivators, such as pain, fear or social rejection.

Stop a behavior one time:
Example: Do not use plastic straws at the restaurant during lunch.

Stopping one-time behaviors is often an early step towards permanent behavior cessation. As you might expect, people are more successful at achieving a one-time stop than making the permanent change. However, even a small step is part of a successful process.

As in decreasing behaviors, the strategies to achieve this cessation are to remove the prompt that leads to the undesirable behavior, reduce the ability to perform the behavior (make it harder to do) and replace the motivation for doing the behavior with de-motivators: pain, fear or social rejection.

Stop a behavior for a period of time:
Example: Do not use the bathtub in the next month.
To stop for a period of time is the prolonged cessation of a behavior. The duration can be short (e.g. four hours), or long (e.g. five weeks). However, the cessation is defined by its continuity. These behaviors are the stepping stones to permanently stop a behavior.
Because the behaviors being stopped are often negative, and sometimes recurrent bad habits, this behavior is one of the most challenging behaviors to induce.
Some strategies to facilitate stopping a behavior are firstly to remove the prompt. If the prompt telling the subject to "do this behavior NOW" is missing, it will not occur. At the same time, the motivation and ability should be reduced. If they are not motivated and do not have the ability any longer, when the prompt occurs the behavior will not be performed. If the task is made harder to perform, or interfered with in some other manner, it is less likely to occur.

Stop a behavior permanently:
Example: Never eat meat again.
This behavior is the ultimate ideal of public sustainable consumption initiatives. As in the previous stop behavior, strategies to cease the performance of the behavior are first of all to remove the prompt. If the prompt telling the subject to "do this behavior NOW" is missing, it will not occur. At the same time, the motivation and ability should be reduced. If they are not motivated and do not have the ability any longer, when the prompt occurs the behavior will not be performed. If the task is made harder to perform, or interfered with in some other manner, it is less likely to occur.

"Design is a needed, necessary and valuable process of invention and innovation, with the potential to take us closer to a sustainable society."

- Chapman and Gant

EVALUATION

ROADMAP

EVALUATION

Eco- efficiency Evaluation
- ☐ Satisfier efficiency
- ☐ Supply/ use efficiency
- ☐ Product efficiency
- ☐ Production efficiency
- ☐ Provision efficiency

Eco- effectiveness Evaluation

☐ Evaluation of critical unsustainable points in the entire life-cycle

☐ Evaluation of possible barriers to sustainable consumer choice in the performance or purchase process

☐ Evaluation of motivation, ability, prompts

After the design team has found ways to implement the desired sustainable behavior through the designed product or service, the next step is to repeatedly test and evaluate various aspects. A series of tests will demonstrate how to improve the intervention and cyclically repeat the map (from defining the behavior to designing concept improvements). These are not scientific tests, but rather quick trials that allow the design team to prototype the design or service experience and see how people react. The team should assess the response ideally by measuring the behavior.

The goal of this evaluation stage is to test and learn what works or does not work in the configuration of the design in order to achieve the performance of the sustainable behavior. The persuasive and sustainable intentions inscribed in the design must be assessed (eco-efficiency and eco-effectiveness, life cycle assessment, possible barriers to achieve the behavior, and evaluation of the ability, motivation and prompts) in order to prove that these specifications are working correctly to achieve the performance of the targeted behavior.

After having the results of the tests and the evaluation, it is possible to iterate. Iterating means modifying the prototype based on feedback until the output is satisfying. A golden rule in the design process is to fail early and often when prototypes and tests are created and to learn from the failures until a successful outcome is achieved. In order to create relevant products, services or interventions that change consumer behavior and promote sustainable consumption, designers must truly understand the consumer's situation, needs, mindset and driving forces. By doing so, designers can ensure that the final result has relevance.

Place sustainability at the center of the design process from idea generation, through implementation, up to the creation of new solutions for complex consumption-related challenges.

MAKE THEM BEHAVE SUSTAINABLY

By following this roadmap during the design process, the tool should assist designers from start to finish in looking for opportunities to introduce potentially new, more sustainable and more effective solutions, remove weak points during the life cycle of products, and bridge the intention-behavior gap.

As with any other design method, there is no absolute right or wrong way to employ sustainable design and consumer behavior change tools and strategies. A successful project involves finding a relevant and workable combination that can conceptualize, develop and prototype ideas through an iterative process of gradual improvement.

It is important to acknowledge that the structure of the tool has a cyclical approach. This means that at every stage of the design process, it might be necessary to take a step back or even start again from scratch or consider the lessons learned and reformulate the targeted behavior to be sure that the outcome will be sustainable.

Download for free the ***Designing Sustainable Consumption Roadmap*** template at www.makethembehave.com and start designing more sustainable interventions.

CASES

interventions that are doing well

11
CASES
THAT ARE
DOING
WELL

The following 11 cases exemplify differing processes and approaches used in practice to achieve consumer behavior change towards sustainable consumption and explore the environmental and social impacts achieved with the interventions.

The examples range from governmental strategies to private services, and from small- to large-scale ventures in order to demonstrate various capabilities of design for sustainable consumption.

MAKE THEM BEHAVE SUSTAINABLY

1. Responsible consumption of plastic bags in Colombia
Colombia

2. Thursday Veggie Day in Ghent
Belgium

3. Sweden Repair Incentive
Sweden

4. Patagonia
US

5. The Keeper Menstrual Cup
US

6. FairPhone
Netherlands

7. Original Unverpackt
Germany

8. Freiluftsupermarkt
Germany

9. Recup
Germany

10. Partago
Belgium

11. wagnisArt
Germany

Responsible consumption of plastic bags in Colombia. ReemBÓLSAle al planeta campaign

Colombia

Governamental strategy

Worldwide, every minute, one million plastic bags are used. In Colombia, between 13 and 14 billion plastic bags are produced and sold every year. Most of them are given free of charge to customers in shops and supermarkets. It is estimated that every Colombian uses an average of six plastic bags per day and 22,176 bags on average over a life of 77 years.

Each plastic bag is used for approximately 20 minutes, but they can take hundreds of years to decompose. Only 5% of them are recycled; the vast majority end up in rivers and oceans, affecting ecosystems, fauna and flora.

However, the impact of the plastic bags is not only in the pollution derived from the final destination after their use: landfills or water sources. The damage to the environment that occurs during their production is also enormous. Producing 100 million plastic bags requires approximately 430 thousand gallons of oil. Every year, around 100 million barrels of oil are used around the world to make plastic bags. In addition, making the plastic used for the bags generates toxic gases, such as sulfur oxide, hydrocarbons, and carbon monoxide, in addition to the 2.09 kilograms of CO_2 generated by the production of one ton of plastic bags.

In 2016, the Ministry of Environment and Sustainable Development of Colombia launched Resolution 668 of 2016, which regulates the rational use of plastic bags. Since the resolution came into force, retailers, supermarkets, shops, and stores must charge consumers a minimum tax for plastic bags. The tax will progressively increase. The initial amount was established in negotiations with the plastics industry so that they could improve their production and find alternatives. It started at 20 cents per bag and will increase to 50, adding 10 cents each year.

Additionally, establishments that provide plastic bags must comply with the four pillars of the resolution: only allow the circulation of bags measuring over 30 x 30 centimeters; the gauge of the bags must be at least 0.9 mm or strong enough to support enough weight without breaking; they should have a message that refers to recycling the bags; and finally, retailers should provide alternatives to transport their products, such as boxes and cloth or paper bags.

Besides the resolution, the Ministry of Environment and Sustainable Development and WWF, together with strategic allies, launched a national strategy called Reem-BÓLSAle al Planeta that seeks to promote the responsible consumption of plastic bags through three main actions: rationalization, reuse, and return of plastic bags for recycling. The main objective is to raise the awareness of the Colombian population about the implications of the consumption and post-consumption of plastic bags, from the beginning to the end of their life cycle.

The campaign started with the launch of the 'día sin bolsa' (day without plastic bags). On this day, medium and large establishments voluntarily committed to not give plastic bags to shoppers at all – not even if they were willing to pay the tax for it. The strategy had good acceptance from establishments and consumers and reduced the usual distribution of plastic bags by approximately 90%.

The campaign was backed by other actions and interventions, social media publications, and the support and commitment of the establishments. In 2016, one of the biggest hardware chain stores in the country saved 5,577,150 bags as part of the campaign.

In 2018, more than 22,000 people registered with the campaign to receive the newsletter and reminders of the campaign with tips on how to consume more sustainably and maintain a more sustainable lifestyle. Some of the active consumers that participated in the campaign won a trip to scuba dive in the Caribbean, where they learned about and saw firsthand the negative impact of plastic bags on marine ecosystems. The intention of the contest was to reward sustainable consumers, as well as provide real information and experiences to create ambassadors for the intervention. In the first six months of implementation, according to the Colombian plastics industry, the use of plastic bags in the country was reduced by 27%.

The tax scheme for plastic bags and governmental actions for their rational use are not new. In fact, it has been applied in more than 120 countries around the world. This taxation started in Denmark back in 1993. Many countries like Denmark, Ireland, Wales, Italy, Scotland, Germany, England, France, Belgium, Mexico, Brazil and Bangladesh, among others, are implementing governmental strategies that range from taxes to banning measures to promote the rational and responsible use of plastic bags. In France, for instance, there is a ban on giving or selling plastic bags that are not biodegradable. In Senegal, the production, importation, sale and distribution of plastic bags is prohibited. South America, Brazil, Uruguay, Argentina, and Chile have already taken measures to control the use of plastic bags as well.

"We have seen in the last year a change in the consumer behavior thanks to campaigns like ReemBÓLSAle al Planeta that without a doubt have a very positive impact on reducing the environmental impact of waste like plastic."

Luis Gilberto Murillo,
Colombian Minister of the Environment
and Sustainable Development

Project **Thursday Veggie Day in Ghent- EVA**

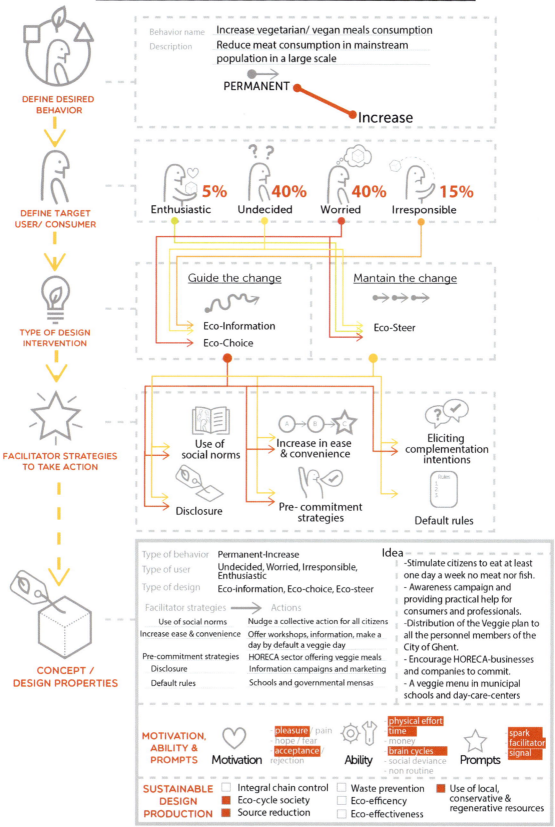

DEFINE DESIRED BEHAVIOR

Behavior name Increase vegetarian/ vegan meals consumption
Description Reduce meat consumption in mainstream population in a large scale

PERMANENT → Increase

DEFINE TARGET USER/ CONSUMER

Enthusiastic 5% Undecided 40% Worried 40% Irresponsible 15%

TYPE OF DESIGN INTERVENTION

Guide the change
Eco-Information
Eco-Choice

Mantain the change
Eco-Steer

FACILITATOR STRATEGIES TO TAKE ACTION

Use of social norms

Increase in ease & convenience

Eliciting complementation intentions

Disclosure

Pre- commitment strategies

Default rules

CONCEPT / DESIGN PROPERTIES

Type of behavior	Permanent-Increase
Type of user	Undecided, Worried, Irresponsible, Enthusiastic
Type of design	Eco-information, Eco-choice, Eco-steer

Idea
- Stimulate citizens to eat at least one day a week no meat nor fish.
- Awareness campaign and providing practical help for consumers and professionals.
- Distribution of the Veggie plan to all the personnel members of the City of Ghent.
- Encourage HORECA-businesses and companies to commit.
- A veggie menu in municipal schools and day-care-centers

Facilitator strategies →	Actions
Use of social norms	Nudge a collective action for all citizens
Increase ease & convenience	Offer workshops, information, make a day by default a veggie day
Pre-commitment strategies	HORECA sector offering veggie meals
Disclosure	Information campaigns and marketing
Default rules	Schools and governmental mensas

MOTIVATION, ABILITY & PROMPTS

Motivation
- pleasure / pain
- hope / fear
- acceptance / rejection

Ability
- physical effort
- time
- money
- brain cycles
- social deviance
- non routine

Prompts
- spark
- facilitator
- signal

SUSTAINABLE DESIGN PRODUCTION
☐ Integral chain control
■ Eco-cycle society
■ Source reduction
☐ Waste prevention
☐ Eco-efficency
☐ Eco-effectiveness
■ Use of local, conservative & regenerative resources

Thursday Veggie Day in Ghent

Belgium

Governamental strategy – Community action

Foto credit: EVA

The Food and Agricultural Organization of the United Nations (FAO) has assessed that 18% of greenhouse gas (GHG) emissions are caused by animal farming. Globally, 115,000 animals are killed for consumption every minute, a figure expected to double by 2050.

According to the FAO, meat consumption "should be a major policy focus when dealing with issues of land degradation, climate change and air pollution, water shortage and water pollution and loss of biodiversity." However, even if the negative impact is visible for most people, eating less meat is almost an unreachable challenge due to food habits, ease, traditional and cultural aspects, commodity or lack of information.

The city of Ghent eases this challenge with a supportive and educational campaign. EVA (Ethical Vegetarian Alternative, Belgium's biggest vegetarian organization) together with the Ghent government launched the Thursday Veggie Day campaign in 2009 and it is still running today. The campaign wants to stimulate the broader public to eat no meat or fish at least one day a week due to the high number of meat-related environmental issues. This initiative consists of both an awareness campaign and the provision of practical help for consumers and professionals to shift towards a vegan diet through workshops, consulting, etc.

The Board of Mayor and Deputy-Mayors of the city decided to support the Thursday Veggie Day campaign, starting at the level of the city of Ghent. The entire municipality backed the project.

The initiative was adopted by citizens in several domains. Individual municipal services have been informed and encouraged to participate in the initiative, i.e., through the distribution of the Veggie Plan to all the staff members of the City of Ghent, lunch discussions about Thursday Veggie Day, and the extension of the vegetarian offerings in the staff restaurant. Also, many HORECA-businesses and companies were encouraged to participate and made a commitment to the Thursday Veggie Day. In October of that year, Thursday Veggie Day was introduced in the municipal schools and daycare centers in Ghent. Since then, all children between 18 months and 12 years have been served a warm vegetarian lunch on Thursdays.

EVA and Ghent have managed to inspire other cities to take part. Many Belgian cities, including Brussels, Antwerp and Hasselt, have also instigated a meatless day. As a result of the campaign, in early 2018, 80% of Ghent residents know about the Veggie Thursday campaign and 31% participated in changing their meat consumption habits. As a consequence, 15% of the population is eating vegetarian meals at least three times a week. Recent data from a poll from January 2018 indicates that 6.6% of citizens changed their diet to a vegetarian or vegan diet and 60% of the population is already aware and thinks it is indeed necessary to eat less meat in the future.

However, EVA recognizes that in order to fight climate change, more than one veggie day per week and the reduction of dairy and animal-based products is also needed. That is why they are now helping people adopt a plant-based diet (vegan) with a campaign called 'Try Vegan,' which is a four-week coaching program.

The Veggie Thursday campaign won the Big Prize for Future Generations Award in 2009 and the Food and Health Award for Best Project in 2008.

The Thursday Veggie Day campaign is a clear example of how governments, without installing taxation or premiums measures, can change consumer behavior on a large scale. The campaign had no legislation involved, but emphasized awareness-raising using different nudging techniques. The campaign focuses the efforts on two main target groups: restaurants and caterers (food providers) and civil populations (consumers). For each group, in order to meet the goal of the campaign, the strategies and tools applied were different, but the main strategic goal for both was the same: to make the 'default option' a vegetarian dish for consumers to easily (and by default) reduce their meat consumption, start acting more sustainably, and contribute to the prevention of climate change.

Traditionally, vegetarian and animal rights organizations reason like this: 'We'll give them all the info on the number of animals killed, number of trees cut... and they'll turn vegetarian.' What if it's the other way round? We make people taste good vegetarian food first, and then they will at least be more open to listen to the arguments for vegetarian food.

Tobias Leenaert, EVA CoFounder

Project **Thursday Veggie Day in Ghent- EVA**

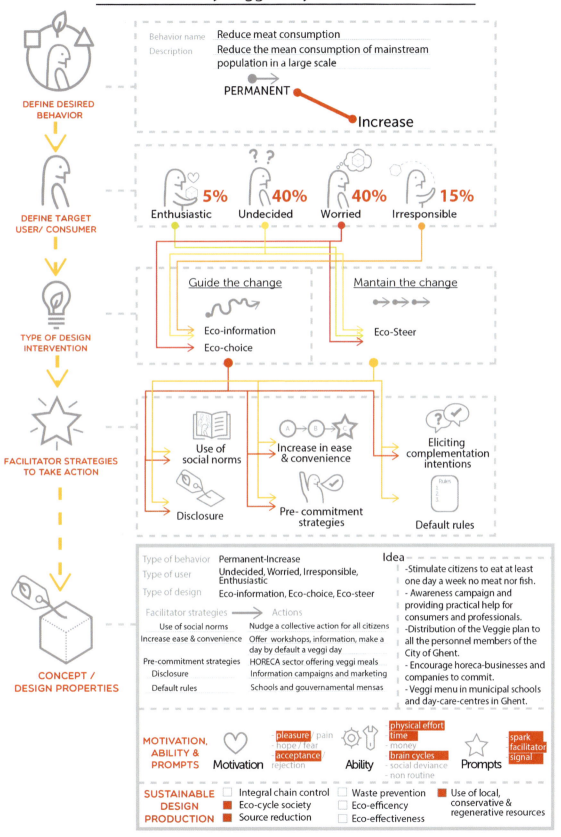

DEFINE DESIRED BEHAVIOR

Behavior name **Reduce meat consumption**
Description **Reduce the mean consumption of mainstream population in a large scale**

PERMANENT

Increase

DEFINE TARGET USER/ CONSUMER

5% Enthusiastic   40% Undecided   40% Worried   15% Irresponsible

TYPE OF DESIGN INTERVENTION

Guide the change
Eco-information
Eco-choice

Mantain the change
Eco-Steer

FACILITATOR STRATEGIES TO TAKE ACTION

Use of social norms

Increase in ease & convenience

Eliciting complementation intentions

Disclosure

Pre- commitment strategies

Default rules

CONCEPT / DESIGN PROPERTIES

Type of behavior	Permanent-Increase
Type of user	Undecided, Worried, Irresponsible, Enthusiastic
Type of design	Eco-information, Eco-choice, Eco-steer

Facilitator strategies →	Actions
Use of social norms	Nudge a collective action for all citizens
Increase ease & convenience	Offer workshops, information, make a day by default a veggi day
Pre-commitment strategies	HORECA sector offering veggi meals
Disclosure	Information campaigns and marketing
Default rules	Schools and gouvernamental mensas

Idea
-Stimulate citizens to eat at least one day a week no meat nor fish.
- Awareness campaign and providing practical help for consumers and professionals.
-Distribution of the Veggie plan to all the personnel members of the City of Ghent.
- Encourage horeca-businesses and companies to commit.
- Veggi menu in municipal schools and day-care-centres in Ghent.

MOTIVATION, ABILITY & PROMPTS

Motivation
- pleasure / pain
- hope / fear
- acceptance / rejection

Ability
- physical effort
- time
- money
- brain cycles
- social deviance
- non routine

Prompts
- spark
- facilitator
- signal

SUSTAINABLE DESIGN PRODUCTION

☐ Integral chain control   ☐ Waste prevention   ☐ Use of local,
■ Eco-cycle society   ☐ Eco-efficency   conservative &
■ Source reduction   ☐ Eco-effectiveness   regenerative resources

Sweden Repair incentive

Sweden

Governamental strategy

In a world of consumerism and mountainous landfills of castoffs, little attention has been paid to the amount of emissions associated with the consumption of goods and services. In 2013, Americans generated about 254 million tons of trash, equivalent to 2 kg per person per day. Similarly, in 2015, Sweden generated 447 kg per capita of municipal solid waste.

Legislators in Sweden proposed a tax break to encourage people to fix things instead of throwing them away. The new rule took effect in January 2017, with the goal of decreasing waste in landfills all over the world, especially in Sweden, which are filling up at an alarming rate.

The legislation works with two types of incentives. The first is to lower the VAT from 25% to 12% on repair services for bicycles, shoes, leather goods, clothing and household linen, for example, to lower the cost of the repair services substantially.
The other scheme is to allow people to claim back from their income tax half of the labor cost of repairs to appliances, such as refrigerators, ovens, dishwashers and washing machines.
Besides the ecological impact of the reduction of waste, Per Bolund, Sweden's Minister for Financial Markets and Consumer Affairs, says that the new law will put more Swedes to work repairing things and lead to the creation of a new home repairs service industry, providing much-needed jobs for new immigrants who lack formal education and consequently reactivating a new sector of the economy.

The government is also planning on introducing a new 'chemicals tax' on white goods and computers to recoup costs for items that are difficult to recycle.
The government has also set aside 4.4 million euros for campaigns to publicize the plan and push recycling.
The incentives are part of a nudging strategy to help the private and municipal sectors make it easier for consumers to act responsibly and reduce their environmental impact with everyday choices.

My hope is also that the opposition parties will see that this is a very good way to both lower the emissions and the environmental effect of consumption and, at the same time, actually create jobs in the repairing businesses.

- Per Bolund, Minister for Financial Markets and Consumer Affairs

MAKE THEM BEHAVE SUSTAINABLY

Project — **Sweden Repair incentive**

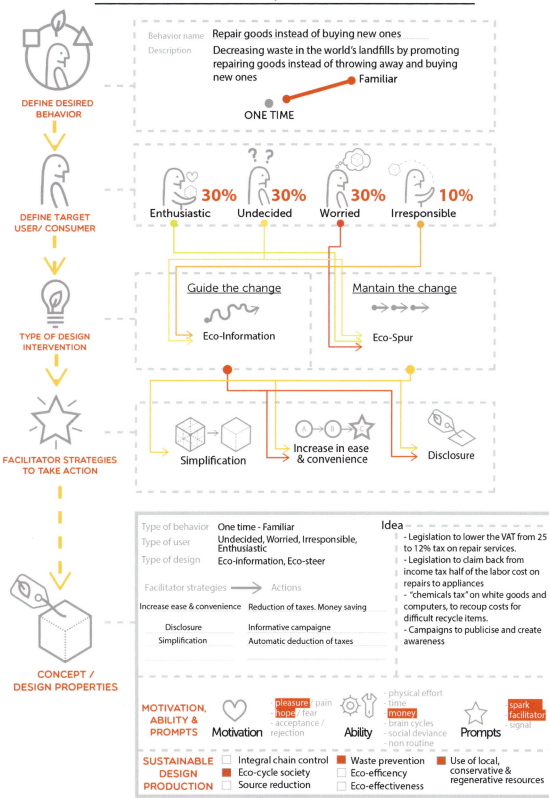

DEFINE DESIRED BEHAVIOR

Behavior name — Repair goods instead of buying new ones
Description — Decreasing waste in the world's landfills by promoting repairing goods instead of throwing away and buying new ones

Familiar

ONE TIME

DEFINE TARGET USER/ CONSUMER

30% Enthusiastic 30% Undecided 30% Worried 10% Irresponsible

TYPE OF DESIGN INTERVENTION

Guide the change — Eco-Information
Mantain the change — Eco-Spur

FACILITATOR STRATEGIES TO TAKE ACTION

Simplification Increase in ease & convenience Disclosure

CONCEPT / DESIGN PROPERTIES

Type of behavior — One time - Familiar
Type of user — Undecided, Worried, Irresponsible, Enthusiastic
Type of design — Eco-information, Eco-steer

Facilitator strategies → Actions

Facilitator strategies	Actions
Increase ease & convenience	Reduction of taxes. Money saving
Disclosure	Informative campaigne
Simplification	Automatic deduction of taxes

Idea
- Legislation to lower the VAT from 25 to 12% tax on repair services.
- Legislation to claim back from income tax half of the labor cost on repairs to appliances
- "chemicals tax" on white goods and computers, to recoup costs for difficult recycle items.
- Campaigns to publicise and create awareness

MOTIVATION, ABILITY & PROMPTS

Motivation
- pleasure / pain
- hope / fear
- acceptance / rejection

Ability
- physical effort
- time
- money
- brain cycles
- social deviance
- non routine

Prompts
- spark
- facilitator
- signal

SUSTAINABLE DESIGN PRODUCTION

☐ Integral chain control   ■ Waste prevention   ■ Use of local, conservative & regenerative resources
■ Eco-cycle society   ☐ Eco-efficency
☐ Source reduction   ☐ Eco-effectiveness

The Keeper Menstrual Cup

US

Business Model- Marketing strategy-
Product development

Every month, about half of the adult population experiences a period as part of their menstruation cycle, requiring them to use feminine hygiene products. The average woman uses roughly 11,000 disposable tampons in her lifetime.

Tampons are used today by over 100 million women worldwide. "Approximately 55% of white women of reproductive age, 31% of black women, and 22% of Hispanic women report using tampons," while pads, which are much more widespread on a global scale due to a cultural aversion to tampons in many regions, represent a multi-billion dollar industry.

Tampons and pads are both produced with materials and processes that are harmful to the environment and personal health.

A package of tampons or pads is composed of the product itself, an applicator (in the case of tampons), the wrapper that holds each individual product, and the packaging that holds all of them. None of these items are reusable or recyclable, so after their brief use they end up as waste in landfills. "The average woman throws away up to 146 kg of feminine hygiene-related products in a lifetime." according to Branch, F. et al. (2015)

In addition to the amount of waste produced, it takes a single tampon (not including the applicator or the packaging), in the best cases, up to six months to decompose, and even longer when they are in a plastic wrapper or bag. The absorbent core itself, specifically the cotton fibers used in the production of tampons, contributes 80% of their total impact. The processing is also resource-intensive, as the farming of cotton requires large amounts of water, pesticides and fertilizer.

Nowadays, there are sustainable alternatives on the market; the menstrual cup is one of them. The cup is a reusable and non-disposable solution designed to catch the menstrual flow, rather than absorb it, with the purpose of, after removal, emptying it, cleaning it and using it again.

In the USA, the first prototypes of menstrual cups were patented in the 1960s and 1970s, but they were not commercially available. In 1987, after more than ten years with no menstrual cup being produced and commercialized, The Keeper, Inc., a woman-owned business, began manufacturing a new latex rubber menstrual cup in the United States. This was the first commercially viable menstrual cup and it is still available today.

The Keeper produces menstrual cups made from latex or medical-grade silicone. The cup is reusable for up to ten years. The company's innovation is backed by its sustainable business values: 'NO BOX, NO LOGO, NO NONSENSE.' All their individual orders are sold and shipped without a box to eliminate unnecessary packaging and printed material. Both the cup and the fabric bag are logo-free and the company does not sell any kind of unnecessary cleaning solution or accessories. Women are growing more and more concerned about the environment and their ecological impact, and the menstrual cup is helping them reevaluate every aspect of their purchasing power of feminine hygiene products. This behavior change, in the long run, is reducing a significant contribution to landfill volume, pollution and health problems.

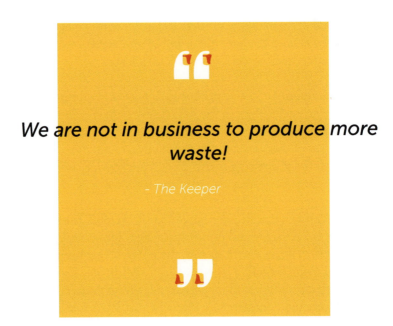

We are not in business to produce more waste!

- The Keeper

The Keeper Menstrual Cup

Project

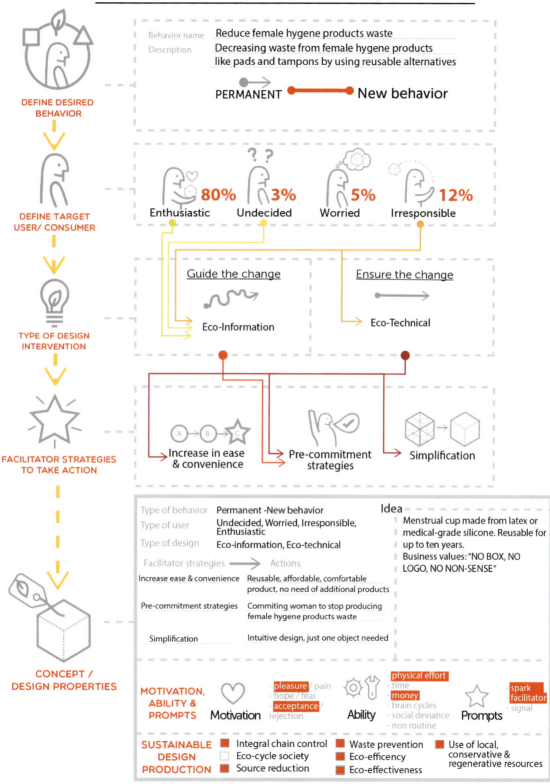

DEFINE DESIRED BEHAVIOR

Behavior name: Reduce female hygene products waste
Description: Decreasing waste from female hygene products like pads and tampons by using reusable alternatives

PERMANENT ⟶ New behavior

DEFINE TARGET USER/ CONSUMER

Enthusiastic 80%   Undecided 3%   Worried 5%   Irresponsible 12%

TYPE OF DESIGN INTERVENTION

Guide the change — Eco-Information

Ensure the change — Eco-Technical

FACILITATOR STRATEGIES TO TAKE ACTION

Increase in ease & convenience   Pre-commitment strategies   Simplification

CONCEPT / DESIGN PROPERTIES

Type of behavior: Permanent -New behavior
Type of user: Undecided, Worried, Irresponsible, Enthusiastic
Type of design: Eco-information, Eco-technical

Facilitator strategies ⟶ Actions

Increase ease & convenience: Reusable, affordable, comfortable product, no need of additional products

Pre-commitment strategies: Commiting woman to stop producing female hygene products waste

Simplification: Intuitive design, just one object needed

Idea
Menstrual cup made from latex or medical-grade silicone. Reusable for up to ten years.
Business values: "NO BOX, NO LOGO, NO NON-SENSE"

MOTIVATION, ABILITY & PROMPTS

Motivation: pleasure / pain, - hope / fear, acceptance / rejection

Ability: physical effort, - time, money, - brain cycles, - social deviance, - non routine

Prompts: spark facilitator, - signal

SUSTAINABLE DESIGN PRODUCTION
- Integral chain control
- Eco-cycle society
- Source reduction
- Waste prevention
- Eco-efficency
- Eco-effectiveness
- Use of local, conservative & regenerative resources

Fairphone

Netherlands

Business Model– Marketing strategy–
Product development

Foto credit: Fairphone

Today, two out of three people worldwide aged 18-35 own a smartphone. In Germany alone, the amount of people in that age group using smartphones is up to almost 92%. Since 2007, 7.1 billion smartphones have been produced due to the low use tendency of a phone (only 12 to 18 months). Increasingly, smartphone manufacturers are forcing consumers to buy new phones or mobile devices after only two years by making products with a shorter lifespan – so-called 'planned obsolescence.' This accelerated and short life cycle of smartphones has a very high cost in various respects. Manufacturing an ordinary mobile phone is estimated to cause 16 kg of CO_2 equivalent emissions, nearly the same as 1 kg of beef. With the power it consumes over two years, that cost rises to 22 kg. More than 60 different elements are commonly used in the manufacturing of smartphones. While the amount of each element in a single device may seem small, the combined impacts of mining and processing these precious materials for 7 billion devices is significant. In addition to the emissions of production and power, the current design of smartphones makes disassembly difficult, including the use of proprietary screws and glued-in batteries; therefore, smartphones are often shredded and sent for smelting when 'recycled' or they end up in a landfill. As a consequence of this inefficient and ineffective process of recovering many of the materials, each device contributes significantly to the 50 million metric tons of e-waste expected to be generated in 2017.

The disposal of cellphones leaves a toxic imprint on the environment because printed circuit boards contain toxic metals, including lead, nickel and beryllium; liquid crystal displays contain mercury; batteries may contain nickel and cadmium; and plastics may contain brominated flame retardants, which are toxic and persist in the environment. Studies suggest that they accumulate in household dust and in the food chain, and have even been detected in some fish. All these substances and materials are hazardous and harmful to both human health and the environment.

Within just one decade, the production and disposal of smartphones have had an enormous impact on both our environment and the widening gaps of social inequality around the world. According to a recent Greenpeace report, workers in manufacturing countries are experiencing slave-like conditions as they mine for minerals or work in production plants to ensure that those with the means have the required unlimited supply of these advanced technologies.
Most likely, the cycle of smartphone production begins in a remote mine in the Democratic Republic of the Congo (DRC). In a country blighted by conflict minerals, over 50% of mines are controlled by armed groups or violent, independent militias. In these cases, the local mining populations experience human rights abuses. Women and girls are regularly sexually abused and brutalized as militias move into mining areas. Making an average of 1 USD a day in an environment lacking in health or safety standards, workers as young as 10 years old dig for tin, tantalum and tungsten. These mineral ores (the 3Ts), in addition to gold, happen to be the fundamental elements in the production of smartphones.

Motivated by making a change in the cellphone sector to improve this situation, a movement for fairer electronics started in 2013 with the foundation of Fairphone.

The social enterprise company aims to develop smartphones that are designed and produced with minimal environmental impact and to put ethical values first.
The company is based in Amsterdam, Netherlands and was founded to develop a mobile device that does not contain conflict minerals, typically gold, tin, tantalum and tungsten. They promote fair labor conditions for the workforce along the supply chain producing the phones and help customers use their phone longer.
The company is making a positive impact and is changing consumer behavior thanks to its approach in four key areas: long-lasting design, fair materials, good working conditions, and reuse and recycling.

Long-lasting Design:
The company is focusing on longevity and reparability to extend the phone's usable life through original design and the ease and convenience of DIY repair by using easily exchangeable modules and parts, giving users more control over their products. Fairphone offers affordable spare parts and helpful tutorials to make it easy for any customer to fix the most commonly broken parts.

Fair Materials:
Fairphone wants to source materials that are less hazardous or toxic with the support of local economies, not armed militias. They're starting with conflict-free minerals from the DRC.

Good Working Conditions:
Fairphone is working closely with manufacturers that want to invest in employee well-being. The company works with a variety of stakeholders (production partners, labor rights experts, NGOs, and researchers) to develop innovative programs to improve worker satisfaction and representation.

Reuse and Recycle:
Fairphone is addressing the full lifespan of mobile phones, including use, reuse and safe recycling. The company wants to use recycled materials in its phones whenever possible.

Project

Fairphone

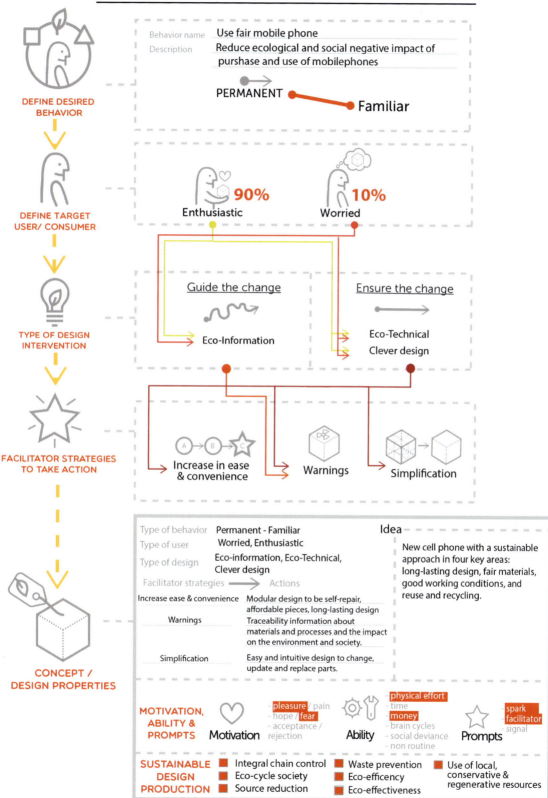

Behavior name Use fair mobile phone
Description Reduce ecological and social negative impact of purshase and use of mobilephones

PERMANENT — Familiar

90% Enthusiastic   10% Worried

Guide the change
Eco-Information

Ensure the change
Eco-Technical
Clever design

FACILITATOR STRATEGIES TO TAKE ACTION
Increase in ease & convenience   Warnings   Simplification

Type of behavior Permanent - Familiar
Type of user Worried, Enthusiastic
Type of design Eco-information, Eco-Technical, Clever design
Facilitator strategies → Actions
Increase ease & convenience Modular design to be self-repair, affordable pieces, long-lasting design
Warnings Traceability information about materials and processes and the impact on the environment and society.
Simplification Easy and intuitive design to change, update and replace parts.

Idea
New cell phone with a sustainable approach in four key areas: long-lasting design, fair materials, good working conditions, and reuse and recycling.

MOTIVATION, ABILITY & PROMPTS

Motivation
- pleasure / pain
- hope / fear
- acceptance / rejection

Ability
- physical effort
- time
- money
- brain cycles
- social deviance
- non routine

Prompts
- spark
- facilitator
- signal

SUSTAINABLE DESIGN PRODUCTION
Integral chain control
Eco-cycle society
Source reduction
Waste prevention
Eco-efficency
Eco-effectiveness
Use of local, conservative & regenerative resources

DEFINE DESIRED BEHAVIOR

DEFINE TARGET USER/ CONSUMER

TYPE OF DESIGN INTERVENTION

FACILITATOR STRATEGIES TO TAKE ACTION

CONCEPT / DESIGN PROPERTIES

Patagonia

US

Business Model– Marketing strategy–
Product development

Globalization has made it possible to produce clothing at increasingly lower prices—prices so low that many consumers worldwide consider this clothing to be disposable. Some call it 'fast fashion,' the clothing equivalent of fast food. According to McKinsey & Company, the average consumer bought 60% more clothing in 2014 than in 2000, but kept each garment only half as long.

Fast fashion leaves a major negative social and environmental impact, particularly on those at the bottom of the supply chain of the clothing life cycle.

For example, polyester, one of the most widely used manufactured fibers, is made from petroleum. The manufacture of polyester and other synthetic fabrics is an energy-intensive process. It requires large amounts of crude oil and the release of emissions, including volatile organic compounds, particulate matter, and acid gases such as hydrogen chloride, all of which can cause or aggravate respiratory disease, in addition to the GHG emissions of the extraction and processing of the oil.

Similarly, cotton, accounting for about 33% of all fibers found in textiles, requires 2,700 liters of water—the equivalent of what one person drinks in two and a half years—to make one cotton shirt. Cotton farming is also responsible for 24% of insecticides and 11% of pesticides, despite using only about 3% of the world's arable land. Toxic chemicals washing into waterways and entering the ecosystems is becoming a major source of pollution, especially in developing countries.

Besides these two main factors of negative environmental impact, the fashion industry, particularly the fast fashion trend, has a major environmental impact. For instance, on water pollution, it's estimated that around 20% of industrial water pollution in the world comes from the treatment and dyeing of textiles and about 8,000 synthetic chemicals are used to turn raw materials into textiles.

Patagonia, the outdoor clothing & gear brand, acknowledges the major impact of the sector and is always outstanding with its position and philosophy on environmental responsibility.

The concept at the very heart of Patagonia's business is to manufacture, repair and recycle long-lasting products.

Patagonia applies circular economy principles by carefully thinking through each step of the product life cycle. By designing durable products that can be repaired, Patagonia ensures that garments stay in use for as long as possible by providing a lifetime guarantee for all its products. If a product can no longer be repaired, Patagonia will recycle it and reimburse the customer.

Patagonia and its decades-long business model rely on communicating its sustainable message and values effectively with its consumers.

In 2005, Patagonia launched the Common Threads Recycling Program. The goal was to reduce the number of products Patagonia customers purchased by encouraging customers to repair damaged clothing. Patagonia began publishing do-it-yourself fixing guides and garment-repair tutorials, produced in partnership with iFixit, to assist customers in repairing their clothing. Additionally, the Common Threads program created a second-hand market for Patagonia garments that did not fit or that were no longer worn. Patagonia collaborated with eBay to develop a storefront and also created an online marketplace on its main website.

In 2011, Patagonia launched a campaign to dissuade customers from purchasing clothing that they did not really need. On Black Friday weekend (the busiest week for retailers in the US), a memorable full-page advertisement in The New York Times read, "DON'T BUY THIS JACKET." In the ad, Patagonia asked people to think about the environmental impacts of their consumption and to buy less, but better, at higher prices and to reflect before making any purchases.

During the spring of 2015, the company launched a campaign called Worn Wear, with which Patagonia promises to make products that endure and to repair, resell, or recycle them as necessary, while consumers, in turn, pledge to buy only what they need, share what is no longer needed and recycle everything else, aiming to reduce excess consumption.

The sustainability values of Patagonia haven't stopped it from achieving an estimated $710 million in sales. Each year, Patagonia donates 1% of its sales to hundreds of environmental organizations. Since 1985, the company has donated $78 million to environmental causes as a way to compensate for its impact on the environment. Due to Patagonia's commitment to environmental issues, its long track record of sustainable innovation in the industry and embedding the principles of the circular economy into its business strategy, the company won the Accenture Strategy Award for Circular Economy Multinational at the World Economic Forum in Davos, Switzerland, in 2017.

> *For us, we engage with our customers because it's a relationship. They need to understand that, as a brand, we are invested in this responsibility for the product from end to end and we are going to help them at each stage of the process.*
>
> *-Rose Marcario, Chief Executive of Patagonia*

Patagonia

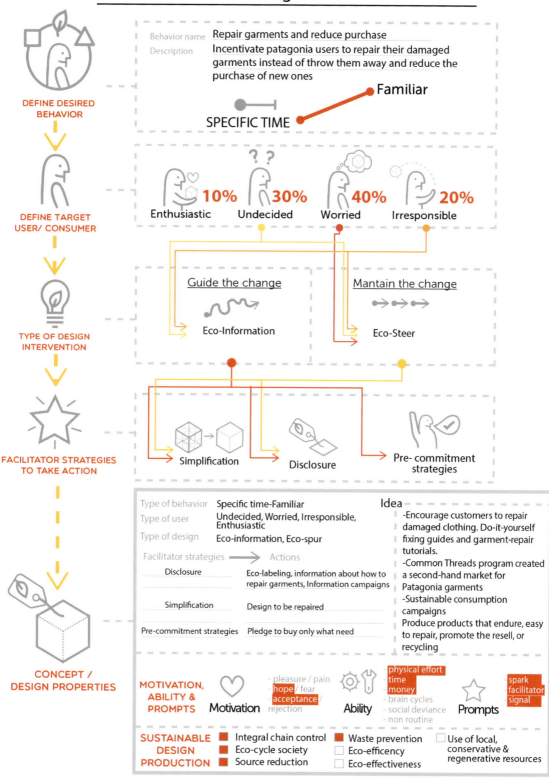

DEFINE DESIRED BEHAVIOR

Behavior name Repair garments and reduce purchase

Description Incentivate patagonia users to repair their damaged garments instead of throw them away and reduce the purchase of new ones

Familiar

SPECIFIC TIME

DEFINE TARGET USER/ CONSUMER

10% Enthusiastic   30% Undecided   40% Worried   20% Irresponsible

TYPE OF DESIGN INTERVENTION

Guide the change — Eco-Information

Mantain the change — Eco-Steer

FACILITATOR STRATEGIES TO TAKE ACTION

Simplification   Disclosure   Pre- commitment strategies

CONCEPT / DESIGN PROPERTIES

Type of behavior Specific time-Familiar
Type of user Undecided, Worried, Irresponsible, Enthusiastic
Type of design Eco-information, Eco-spur

Facilitator strategies ⟶ Actions

Disclosure Eco-labeling, information about how to repair garments, Information campaigns

Simplification Design to be repaired

Pre-commitment strategies Pledge to buy only what need

Idea
- Encourage customers to repair damaged clothing. Do-it-yourself fixing guides and garment-repair tutorials.
- Common Threads program created a second-hand market for Patagonia garments
- Sustainable consumption campaigns
Produce products that endure, easy to repair, promote the resell, or recycling

MOTIVATION, ABILITY & PROMPTS

Motivation
- pleasure / pain
- hope / fear
- acceptance / rejection

Ability
- physical effort
- time
- money
- brain cycles
- social deviance
- non routine

Prompts
- spark
- facilitator
- signal

SUSTAINABLE DESIGN PRODUCTION

■ Integral chain control   ■ Waste prevention   ☐ Use of local, conservative & regenerative resources
■ Eco-cycle society   ☐ Eco-efficency
■ Source reduction   ☐ Eco-effectiveness

Original Unverpackt

Germany

Business Model

One of the biggest challenges of our time is to deal with the overwhelming amount of packaging, principally difficult-to-recycle plastics.

According to the European Commission´s packaging waste statistics, in 2014, 162.9 kg of packaging waste were generated per inhabitant in the 28 member states of the EU. This quantity varied between 48.3 kg per inhabitant in Croatia and 220 kg per inhabitant in Germany. In the same year, 19% of the total amount of waste was plastic. In Germany alone, more than 17 million tons of packaging ends up in the trash each year, which also contributes to 20 million tons of the nation's greenhouse gas emissions annually. It is indeed clear that in regular supermarkets, it is highly difficult for consumers to buy more sustainable and low-packaging options. However, under the banner of 'Zero Waste,' a movement is currently forming. Members have adjusted their personal lifestyles to produce as little trash as possible.

Under this movement, 'Original Unverpackt' (Original Unpackaged) flourished as the first packaging-free supermarket in Germany. Organic food and drinks free of labels and brands are kept in hoppers, jars, bins or bottles, and shoppers are encouraged to bring their own bags and containers with them and pick up just the amount they need. Recycled containers are also available onsite to borrow from the store. The Berlin zero-waste grocery store offers more than 600 products that can be purchased sustainably. The products range from basic food necessities such as bread, eggs, nuts and fruits to luxury foods like chocolate, wine and gin. The store also offers suitable organic cleaning products for both personal use and home cleaning, such as eco dishwashing sponges and cloths made from cotton, soaps, bamboo toothbrushes and ecological laundry soap.

Original Unverpackt helps shoppers not only reduce the amount of packaging bound to end as waste, but also to lower their contribution of CO_2 emissions by choosing organic and locally produced food. Buying in the store implicitly raises awareness of the link between sustainability matters and consumer behavior, making shoppers more critical and empowered towards zero-waste alternatives and sustainable lifestyles. The growing Zero Waste movement – led by both producers and consumers – is showing the retail sector how things could be done differently and it is starting to deliver on the demand for new and innovative solutions that meet their desired sustainable standards.

We created the shop with help from a lot of people. That was new, and people realized that it's really about creating an alternative, about showing the retail sector how things could be done differently. We wanted to inspire others.

- Milena Glimbovski,
Original Unverpackt founder

MAKE THEM BEHAVE SUSTAINABLY

Original Unverpackt

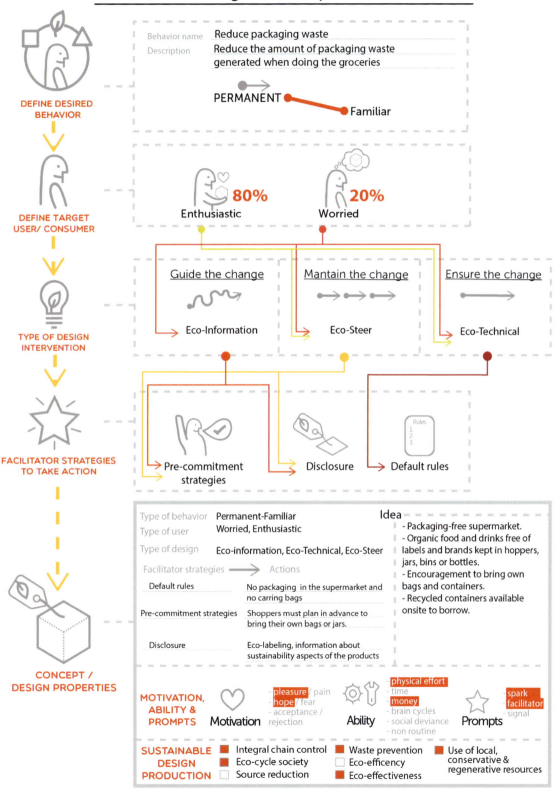

Project

DEFINE DESIRED BEHAVIOR

Behavior name: Reduce packaging waste
Description: Reduce the amount of packaging waste generated when doing the groceries

PERMANENT — Familiar

DEFINE TARGET USER/ CONSUMER

Enthusiastic 80%   Worried 20%

TYPE OF DESIGN INTERVENTION

Guide the change — Eco-Information
Mantain the change — Eco-Steer
Ensure the change — Eco-Technical

FACILITATOR STRATEGIES TO TAKE ACTION

Pre-commitment strategies   Disclosure   Default rules

CONCEPT / DESIGN PROPERTIES

Type of behavior: Permanent-Familiar
Type of user: Worried, Enthusiastic
Type of design: Eco-information, Eco-Technical, Eco-Steer

Facilitator strategies → Actions

Default rules: No packaging in the supermarket and no carring bags

Pre-commitment strategies: Shoppers must plan in advance to bring their own bags or jars.

Disclosure: Eco-labeling, information about sustainability aspects of the products

Idea
- Packaging-free supermarket.
- Organic food and drinks free of labels and brands kept in hoppers, jars, bins or bottles.
- Encouragement to bring own bags and containers.
- Recycled containers available onsite to borrow.

MOTIVATION, ABILITY & PROMPTS

Motivation
- pleasure / pain
- hope / fear
- acceptance / rejection

Ability
- physical effort
- time
- money
- brain cycles
- social deviance
- non routine

Prompts
- spark
- facilitator
- signal

SUSTAINABLE DESIGN PRODUCTION

- Integral chain control
- Eco-cycle society
- Source reduction
- Waste prevention
- Eco-efficency
- Eco-effectiveness
- Use of local, conservative & regenerative resources

Recup

Germany

Business Model- Service

Foto credit: Recup

The consumerist trend of single-use products results in half the plastic produced globally going into products that are used only once, which creates a staggering amount of waste. One of the most recurrent consumption habits around the world that supports this trend is drinking takeaway coffee.

Although most consumers believe the paper cups are reusable and recyclable, less than 1% of takeaway coffee cups get into the recycling processes and thus end up in landfills. Most disposable cups are lined with polyethylene, so they cannot be recycled. The plastic lining also means that they take a long time to break down. Another factor that makes this product have such a major impact is that due to health regulations and paper manufacturing, each cup uses 90% virgin pulp to be produced.

Annually, over 500 billion disposable cups are being manufactured across the globe and are responsible for approximately 125 billion pounds of CO_2. This fact only corresponds to the manufacturing and transport and not the emissions produced once they get into the landfill. Canada and the United States are the main countries responsible for this consuming behavior. It was estimated that in the USA alone, 58 billion disposable cups end up in landfills each year. On a smaller but still alarming scale, Germany uses three billion non-recyclable single-use cups every year, representing some 320,000 takeaway coffee cups across the country every hour. This disposable product promotes a throwaway culture of one-time use that produces CO_2 emissions of around 83,000 tons every year for their production in Germany alone.

To confront this problem, reCUP, a German startup, is establishing a nationwide deposit system (pfandsystem) to offer a reusable takeaway coffee cup service. In Germany, this system is very common in a wide range of services: glasses and plates in biergartens, reusable plastic and glass bottles, car batteries, and printer ink containers. reCUP wants to encourage coffee lovers to consume more sustainably, while maintaining the deep-seated coffee-to-go philosophy.

With over 700 partners (coffee shops, canteens, bakeries, etc.), takeaway coffee consumers can order their daily coffee in their regular establishment and get it in a reusable reCUP. Users of this service place a 1€ deposit which is refunded when the cup is returned (dirty or clean) to any reCUP partner location; they also receive a small discount on their coffee.

By replacing the disposable cups with reusable ones made of polypropylene, each cup can be reused and cleaned around 500 times. Furthermore, the technical properties of the material allow the cups to be recycled many times during their material lifetime, as they can be upcycled or recycled into another product.

reCUP officially launched in Munich, Berlin, Oldenburg, Rosenheim, Wasserburg, Köln and Ludwigsburg, and further cities are to follow. Showing great success, reCUP had more than 160,000 cups in circulation at the beginning of 2018 and convinced 20% of its partners to sell takeaway coffee only in reusable cups, rather than disposable ones. As part of the service, the company offers a free app with updated information to locate the closest and most convenient place to pick up a cup of tasty coffee or drop it off when finished.

Even though we focus on replacing disposable coffee cups, we feel that our action has a larger impact, creating awareness for sustainable use of our resources with a product/service that everyone easily understands.

- Recup

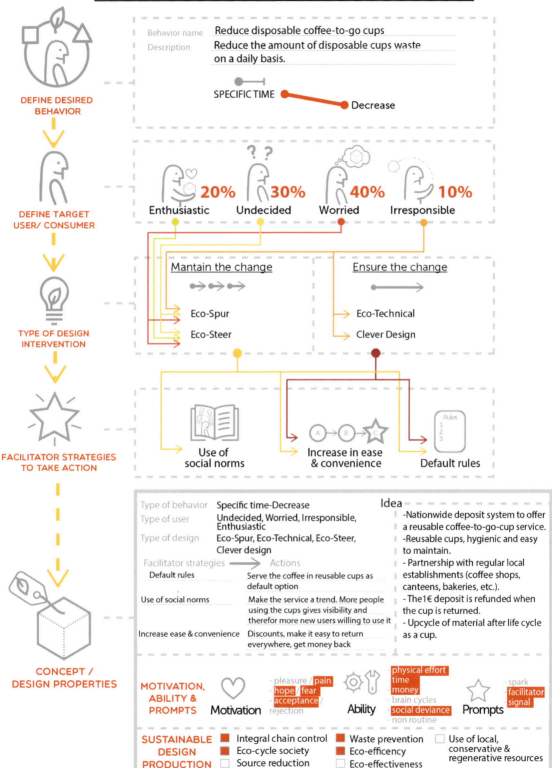

Project

Recup

DEFINE DESIRED BEHAVIOR

Behavior name: Reduce disposable coffee-to-go cups
Description: Reduce the amount of disposable cups waste on a daily basis.

SPECIFIC TIME — Decrease

DEFINE TARGET USER/ CONSUMER

Enthusiastic **20%**   Undecided **30%**   Worried **40%**   Irresponsible **10%**

TYPE OF DESIGN INTERVENTION

Mantain the change
→ Eco-Spur
→ Eco-Steer

Ensure the change
→ Eco-Technical
→ Clever Design

FACILITATOR STRATEGIES TO TAKE ACTION

Use of social norms   Increase in ease & convenience   Default rules

Rules
1
2
3

CONCEPT / DESIGN PROPERTIES

Type of behavior	Specific time-Decrease	
Type of user	Undecided, Worried, Irresponsible, Enthusiastic	
Type of design	Eco-Spur, Eco-Technical, Eco-Steer, Clever design	
Facilitator strategies →	Actions	
Default rules	Serve the coffee in reusable cups as default option	
Use of social norms	Make the service a trend. More people using the cups gives visibility and therefor more new users willing to use it	
Increase ease & convenience	Discounts, make it easy to return everywhere, get money back	

Idea
- Nationwide deposit system to offer a reusable coffee-to-go-cup service.
- Reusable cups, hygienic and easy to maintain.
- Partnership with regular local establishments (coffee shops, canteens, bakeries, etc.).
- The 1€ deposit is refunded when the cup is returned.
- Upcycle of material after life cycle as a cup.

MOTIVATION, ABILITY & PROMPTS

Motivation
- pleasure / pain
- hope / fear
- acceptance / rejection

Ability
- physical effort
- time
- money
- brain cycles
- social deviance
- non routine

Prompts
- spark
- facilitator
- signal

SUSTAINABLE DESIGN PRODUCTION

- ◼ Integral chain control
- ◼ Eco-cycle society
- ☐ Source reduction
- ◼ Waste prevention
- ◼ Eco-efficency
- ☐ Eco-effectiveness
- ☐ Use of local, conservative & regenerative resources

Freiluftsupermarkt- bauchplan).(

Germany

Business Model- Service- Community action

Foto credit: cloudjumper/ bauchplan).(

In 1900, worldwide, there were 6.7 rural dwellers for each urban dweller; nowadays, there is less than one. Projections suggest there will be nearly three urban dwellers to every two rural dwellers by 2025. This has been derived from the rapid growth of the population and the world economy. The proportion of gross world product and the economically active population working in industry and services gets higher every day, since most industrial and service enterprises are in urban areas (Satterthwaite et al., 2010).

UN projections suggest that the world's urban population will grow by more than a billion people between 2010 and 2025, while the rural population will hardly grow at all (United Nations, 2008). It is likely that the proportion of the global population not producing food will also continue to grow, as will the number of middle- and upper-income consumers whose dietary choices are more energy- and greenhouse gas emission-intensive (and often more land-intensive). Such changes in demand also bring major changes to agriculture and in the supply chain.

For these reasons, urban planners cannot neglect the importance of a sustainable transition from farming lands into sustainable urban areas in which agricultural values should be kept to cushion the impact of the cessation of agricultural activity in the area.

The city of Munich (Germany) has been undergoing this type of transformation. One of the biggest urban development projects has been underway over recent decades. The development of the western district of Munich, called Freiham, includes plans to transform the area from agricultural fields and green areas into an urban district of the city. Over 25,000 new inhabitants are estimated to live in the area in the coming years.

The municipality decided to financially support a temporary project to reduce the dissatisfaction of current residents and the worries that could emerge from the change. The plan for the transformation of the area keeps the agricultural component to offer transitory functional use of the area, and to address the challenge of the new urban changes by the residents.

The funds were granted to the project Freiluftsupermarkt (FLS), which was conceptualized, planned and developed by the landscape and urban planning studio bauchplan).(.

Based on the urban food strategy Agropolis, which articulates a sustainable food economy to strengthen the awareness of soil as a resource, the FLS is a temporary platform in the designated area that offers transitional and functional alternatives to use the developing territory. The project had two main goals. The first was to draw attention to the new urban development to make it accessible during the construction period. On the one hand, this creates a bond between the visitors, the possible new inhabitants and the activities being developed in the area. On the other hand, it creates the possibility to observe the progress and development of Freiham.

The second goal was to link Freiham with food during the development of the district in order to not lose the agricultural identity of the place. The FLS sought to grow the awareness and willingness of the future inhabitants to have agricultural spaces and activities in the district and to incorporate agriculture and food into urban daily life (on rooftops, facades, courtyards, etc.) to stimulate local consumption of agri-products and encourage closed-loop economies.

The core of the intervention was a community-urban-agriculture garden under the 'pick your own' system (people harvest what they want to buy and leave the money in a box near the fields). The garden supports the engagement of residents with the idea of self-sufficiency through the transition process of the territory, keeping urban agriculture practices as the driver of the development of the territory. The FLS gave residents the opportunity to take part in the urban development process, resulting in the development of local initiatives and local activities for the use of the space.

Different open-air events took place in the area to spread information about a variety of topics: urban development, ecology, environment, regionality, sustainable consumption behavior, development progress of the area, agriculture practices, sustainable lifestyle, etc.

In 2016, many stakeholders were involved in the construction process on different levels. With the participation of and work by other partners, local institutions, school classes, and volunteers, including great help from refugees, the structure of the fields was built. This collaboration fortified a community-based action in which the residents felt committed to the project, their neighbors and their neighborhood. The intervention was designed to reach a wide range of people: students, refugees, academics and German citizens, among others. It created a space for cultural recreation that incentivizes citizens to choose a more sustainable lifestyle (bike tours, DIY food production, clean and organic harvest, shortened distances to travel for supplies, etc.).

The transformation of the FLS encouraged consumers to reduce their waste, value the soil and agricultural practices, and also raised awareness about sustainable lifestyles. The knowledge, awareness, and experiences of the people involved in the project extended to their daily lives even after the FLS activities were finished.

The project became a great engine for many social processes in the area of Freiham and its surroundings. The FLS reached different actors in the community and helped them work together. It made them aware of the transition of the rural area of Freiham into an urban neighborhood of Munich, keeping agriculture as the pillar of the transition.

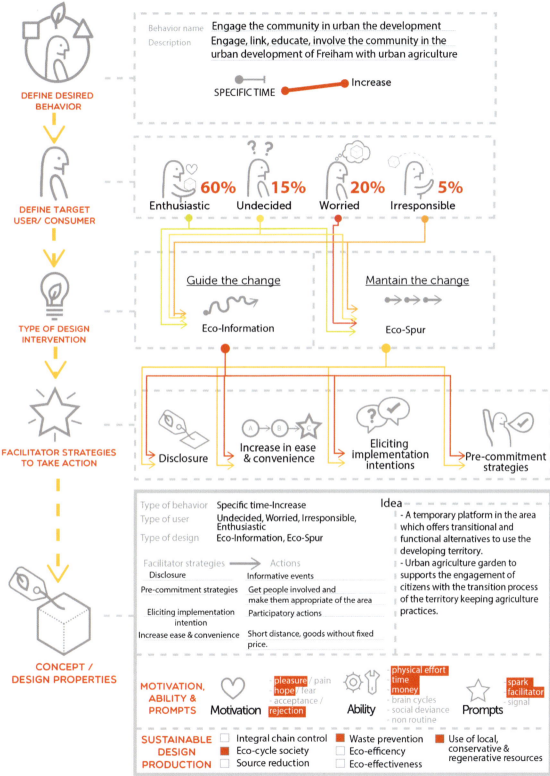

Project **Freiluftsupermarkt**

DEFINE DESIRED BEHAVIOR

Behavior name: Engage the community in urban the development

Description: Engage, link, educate, involve the community in the urban development of Freiham with urban agriculture

SPECIFIC TIME ——— Increase

DEFINE TARGET USER/ CONSUMER

Enthusiastic **60%**   Undecided **15%**   Worried **20%**   Irresponsible **5%**

TYPE OF DESIGN INTERVENTION

Guide the change — Eco-Information

Mantain the change — Eco-Spur

FACILITATOR STRATEGIES TO TAKE ACTION

Disclosure | Increase in ease & convenience | Eliciting implementation intentions | Pre-commitment strategies

CONCEPT / DESIGN PROPERTIES

Type of behavior: Specific time-Increase
Type of user: Undecided, Worried, Irresponsible, Enthusiastic
Type of design: Eco-Information, Eco-Spur

Facilitator strategies	Actions
Disclosure	Informative events
Pre-commitment strategies	Get people involved and make them appropriate of the area
Eliciting implementation intention	Participatory actions
Increase ease & convenience	Short distance, goods without fixed price.

Idea
- A temporary platform in the area which offers transitional and functional alternatives to use the developing territory.
- Urban agriculture garden to supports the engagement of citizens with the transition process of the territory keeping agriculture practices.

MOTIVATION, ABILITY & PROMPTS

Motivation
- pleasure / pain
- hope / fear
- acceptance / rejection

Ability
- physical effort
- time
- money
- brain cycles
- social deviance
- non routine

Prompts
- spark
- facilitator
- signal

SUSTAINABLE DESIGN PRODUCTION

☐ Integral chain control   ■ Waste prevention   ■ Use of local, conservative & regenerative resources
■ Eco-cycle society   ☐ Eco-efficency
☐ Source reduction   ☐ Eco-effectiveness

Partago

Belgium

Business Model- Service

Foto credit: Partago

The carbon dioxide emitted by cars contributes greatly to global warming and climate change. Emissions of NOx lead to air pollution and are harmful to the environment and human health. The global car fleet, the sheer numbers of cars, and the fact that car ownership is deeply ingrained contributes to this persisting phenomenon.

Unsurprisingly, most countries with high car ownership rates in 2014 were regions with advanced economies. In countries like Germany and the US, over 85% of households own a car.

Car ownership has a negative impact on the environment due not only to the emissions produced by petrol and diesel cars, but also to a complex sum of factors. One of these components is the use-inefficiency of car ownership. The total time a car is used in relation to the number of resources used and CO_2 emissions produced in the car's fabrication is extremely low. The production process of a car emits as much carbon pollution as driving it, taking into account that for around 90% of a car's entire lifetime, it sits unused. This fact can be translated into another contributor to the unsustainable use of owned cars: each car occupies 150 m^2 of urban land and is a significant contributor to traffic jams and the occupation of roads. Today, thanks to digitization and the sharing economy, there is an opportunity to reduce the number of privately-owned cars in cities. With the car-sharing business model, users can easily log in, locate the closest shared vehicle available, rent the car for a short period of time (normally per hours or minutes), drive off and drop the car anywhere in the city or return it to its station or zone (area).

One study from the USA indicates that the global car fleet could be reduced by one-third if sharing schemes were widely adopted. Another study in Lisbon shows that just 10% of vehicles could maintain the same level of mobility if shared. Each car-sharing vehicle replaces at least four to eight personal cars on average.

Partago surged as a mobility solution in the city of Ghent in Belgium. It is an innovative car-sharing network with strong sustainability values. Part of its innovative added value is that all the cars are electrical. This aspect reduces CO_2 emissions substantially, along with diminished pollution and noise. Additionally, the company differs from other similar services because Partago is a co-operative founded and financed by citizens. That means that all users become members and own a part of the company. With this innovative solution, Partago ensures that all users and members advocate for the good use, maintenance and sustainability of the company. Partago offers affordable and convenient time bundles to incentivize users to prefer this shared alternative. In 2017, prices ranged from 60 euros for 10 hours of use up to 300 euros for 70 hours.

This price includes the entire service: kilometers driven, insurance, maintenance, charging on the road, and free parking. Consequently, for users that drive less than 10,000 km per year, using the service is more cost-effective than owning a personal car.

Together with the vehicle aspects of environmental relief, the services also actively influence the mobility behavior of customers and support a 'car-light' mobility orientation.

Car-sharing users learn to make better use of the alternatives to vehicle use. They discover, for example, the possibilities of using public transport or getting a better bicycle for day-to-day travel. Some users develop strategies for combining destinations into one journey, rather than making each one individually.

Partago provides a service that requires a lot of behavioral change from most people, so managing this process is key for the success of Partago and the satisfaction of users.

A healthy city requires citizens who can decide together on the most environmentally friendly way to move around. Partago aims just to achieve that. We offer access to our shared electric cars

- Joachim Jacob, Partago Managing Director & Co-Founder

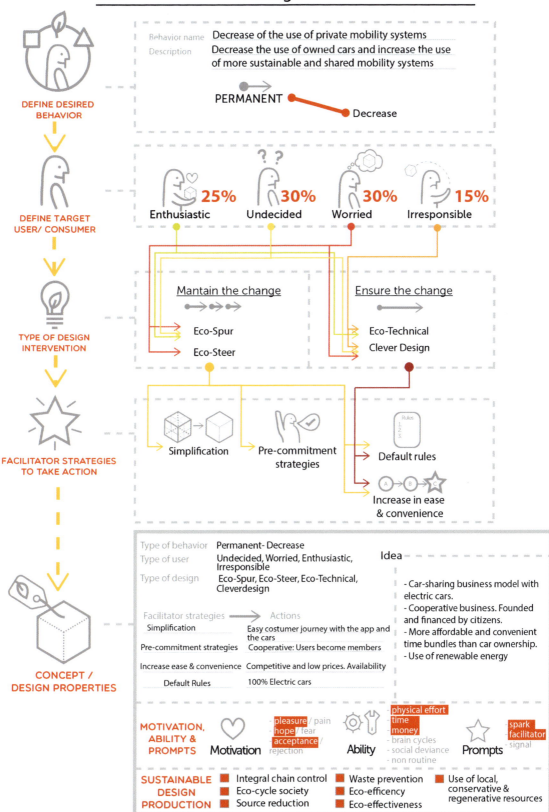

Project

Partago

wagnisART

Germany

Business Model- Service- Community action

Foto credit: David Riek/ bauchplan).

The construction industry is one of the biggest industries worldwide. It makes significant contributions towards social and economic development at the national and international levels. It also provides communities with places for housing, education, culture, healthcare, business, leisure and entertainment. However, at the same time, it is arguably one of the most resource-intensive and environmentally damaging industries worldwide. On the one hand, construction accounts for 40% of the total flow of raw materials into the global economy every year. It is a substantial source of waste, pollution and land dereliction (Earth Watch Institute, 2011; Roodman and Lenssen, 1995). According to studies, the construction sector is responsible for 40% of energy consumption and 50% of total waste generated.

On the other hand, according to the Environmental Protection Agency (EPA), in 2010, 6% of global greenhouse gas emissions derived from the building sector. GHG emissions and indirect emissions from electricity use by homes have increased due to increasing electricity consumption for lighting, heating, air conditioning and appliances.

To reduce the environmental impact of the use phase of buildings, more energy-efficient constructions are needed, together with an increase of the integration, education and participation of householders. Energy-efficient and sustainable building may perform well in theory — based on analytical building models and simulations – but the actual performance of inhabited houses often runs contrary to expectations. History has shown a gap between potential and actual energy savings, often associated with the behavior of the people who use the buildings and building systems. Increasing evidence (e.g., Stern, 2002; Janda, 2014) suggests that the everyday behavior of building occupants and standard operating procedures of organizations are a much-overlooked factor in achieving building performance goals and the conservation of resources (energy, water, materials).

Therefore, the building inhabitants should be involved in the process and be trained or well informed about the building systems and how their behaviors, individually and collectively, affect a building's environmental performance.

Following this principle, the landscape architecture studio bauchplan, together with the cooperation of the architects bogevischs, Udo Schindler and Walter Hable planned, designed and implemented for the German cooperative Wagnis eG the project 'wagnisART' in the city of Munich. The project was awarded the 2016 German Urbanization Prize. It was characterized in particular by its participatory planning process. Future inhabitants and other construction stakeholders of the housing project were involved in the entire process.

The one-hectare project is located in Domagkpark, on the site of the former Funk-kaserne, where one of the biggest artist colonies in Europe has existed since 1993. The main intention of the project was to redesign the area and the remains of the Kunsthof into a housing complex.

The central element of the experimental planning was the community and the future inhabitants.

The project integrated the community from the very beginning, with numerous workshops and planning groups. On the one hand, this process was very successful and enriching because it took future inhabitants' ideas and needs regarding the distribution and purpose of the space, especially of the communal areas, that later on, with the executing partners, were successfully implemented.

On the other hand, the integrative approach worked as a social cohesion tool that made the residents work together in the construction of the area, strengthening the community factor to create unity, reducing costs derived from the workforce.

The result is a residential area with special art and cultural influences, consisting of five sustainable residential buildings connected by bridges on two levels to incentivize community integration. The buildings are erected using sustainable and efficient construction principles following the Passivhaus standards, saving heat, energy and water flows as much as possible. High-isolation material was used to make the building more efficient. Additionally, materials were selected carefully in order to buy and use only what was really needed, both to save money and to produce as little waste as possible.

wagnisART has communal areas and services that give the inhabitants numerous opportunities to interact and develop flexible use of the open areas that make the daily interaction with spaces and the buildings more sustainable. This is the main sustainable factor of the project: to make it possible to have sustainable lifestyles based on the community and residents' needs, wants and desires. Inhabitants decided themselves where to intervene to make the housing complex more sustainable.

As a result, there are rooftops with solar panels for energy generation, roof gardens to grow food and herbs, and shared green areas and flowerbeds for recreation; all of these are part of the wagnisART area.

Community spaces also include courtyards for social interaction, studios, offices, a café, ateliers, a sewing room, guest apartments, and a laundry-cafe.

Having a community laundry room that is also a social space fosters a sense of community and offers an engaging place for residents to meet and have a coffee together. Besides the social component, inhabitants saved space designated for the laundry area in their apartments and lowered initial costs, since fewer washing machines were required and operational costs were reduced.

Similarly, wagnisART offers a special feature, the so-called cluster apartments (Clusterwohnungen). Specifically meant for the elderly, with up to 400 m² of living space, these hybrids between private and communal apartments are composed of up to eight small apartments with a small room, private bathroom and a small kitchenette arranged around a shared living area and a bigger kitchen. This initiative seeks to reduce unused space in large apartments owned by older people or small families and create community support and unity among neighbors.

Another incentive to make the residents of wagnisART behave more sustainably is the use of bikes. With residents' participation during the planning sessions, it was agreed to have more bike parking stands and fewer car spots than regulated. In total, only 50% of the regulatory number of parking spaces was created. This motivates and nudges inhabitants to use alternative mobility means, such as public transportation, car sharing, and especially bikes.

The wagnisART project as an experimental participatory planning process enabled the residents of the area to be more aware and involved in the whole process of building. It became a reference point of sustainable and integrated community housing for people in the city of Munich who are willing to have a more sustainable and community-engaged lifestyle. The planning, construction, maintenance and habits make the residential area of wagnisART a complete success in terms of social, economic and environmental sustainability.

Landscape architecture and especially wagnisART is about creating urban spaces that generate possibilities and encourage sustainable lifestyles in daily life and with one's social and ecological environment.

– bauchplan).(

Project **wagnisART**

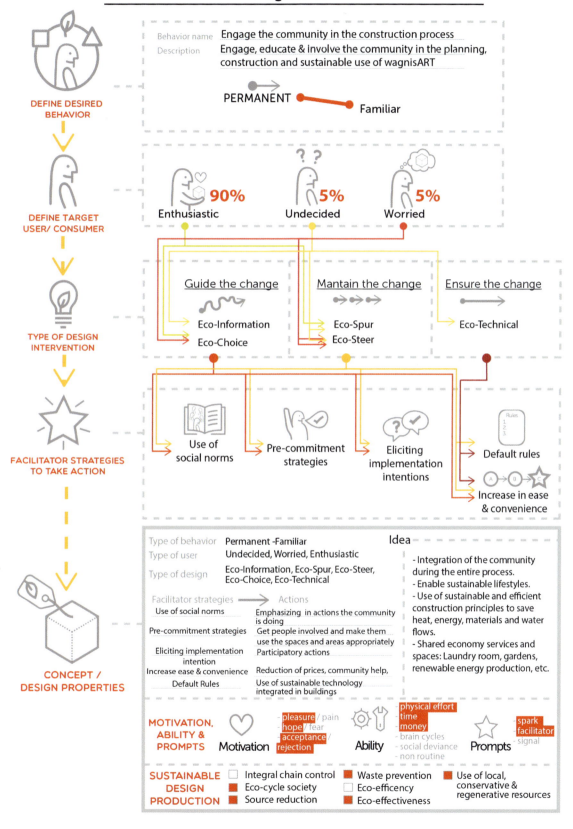

Behavior name — Engage the community in the construction process
Description — Engage, educate & involve the community in the planning, construction and sustainable use of wagnisART

PERMANENT — Familiar

DEFINE DESIRED BEHAVIOR

Enthusiastic **90%**   Undecided **5%**   Worried **5%**

DEFINE TARGET USER/ CONSUMER

Guide the change
Eco-Information
Eco-Choice

Mantain the change
Eco-Spur
Eco-Steer

Ensure the change
Eco-Technical

TYPE OF DESIGN INTERVENTION

Use of social norms
Pre-commitment strategies
Eliciting implementation intentions
Default rules
Increase in ease & convenience

FACILITATOR STRATEGIES TO TAKE ACTION

Idea

Type of behavior — Permanent -Familiar
Type of user — Undecided, Worried, Enthusiastic
Type of design — Eco-Information, Eco-Spur, Eco-Steer, Eco-Choice, Eco-Technical

Facilitator strategies → Actions
Use of social norms — Emphasizing in actions the community is doing
Pre-commitment strategies — Get people involved and make them use the spaces and areas appropriately
Eliciting implementation intention — Participatory actions
Increase ease & convenience — Reduction of prices, community help,
Default Rules — Use of sustainable technology integrated in buildings

- Integration of the community during the entire process.
- Enable sustainable lifestyles.
- Use of sustainable and efficient construction principles to save heat, energy, materials and water flows.
- Shared economy services and spaces: Laundry room, gardens, renewable energy production, etc.

CONCEPT / DESIGN PROPERTIES

MOTIVATION, ABILITY & PROMPTS

Motivation
- pleasure / pain
- hope / fear
- acceptance / rejection

Ability
physical effort
time
money
- brain cycles
- social deviance
- non routine

Prompts
spark
facilitator
- signal

SUSTAINABLE DESIGN PRODUCTION
☐ Integral chain control   ■ Waste prevention   ■ Use of local, conservative & regenerative resources
■ Eco-cycle society   ☐ Eco-efficency
■ Source reduction   ■ Eco-effectiveness

While I worked on this book, I reflected that <u>design for sustainable consumption offers a holistic mindset with a sustainable consumer-centric approach</u>. It helps producers to produce better and consumers to consume better. Designers, the industry and policy makers must reconsider their work and the value they generate from a sustainable perspective. Transforming design approaches, products and services is a major part of the thinking and action required to address sustainable consumption. It is indeed true that design plays an increasingly important role in shaping users' awareness, desires and behaviors.

We are all citizens of the world.
We can all make a positive impact.
The turning point for a sustainable future is to acknowledge it.

The change goes on...

Online Website
Please visit the website: www.makethembehave.com
This site offers the roadmap and a variety of bonus content available for free.

Support the book
If you liked the book and the content was useful to you, I would be grateful if you shared your review of the book on Amazon or wherever you purchased it and tell your friends and share it via your online channels.
Reviews mean a lot to the authors and the success of the book.

Thank you,

Adriana Olaya Rodriguez

What can I do for you?

I am actively looking to collaborate with researchers, policy makers, designers and interested people to help shape the future of business, interventions, and policies.

I am experienced at speaking, training and coaching on the topic of sustainable consumer behavior change. Consider contacting me for any or all of the following:

- Deliver personal sustainable consumer behavior change consulting

- Co-create sustainable consumer behavior change interventions

- Lead a workshop with your organization

Organizations cited

bauchplan, www.bauchplan.de

Patagonia, www.patagonia.com

Ministry of Environmental and Sustainable Development of Colombia, www.minambiente.gov.co/

Soy eColombiano, www.soyecolombiano.com/

EVA, https://www.evavzw.be

Ministry of Finance and Consumption of Sweden, http://www.government.se/

The Keeper, https://keeper.com/

FairPhone, https://www.fairphone.com

Original Unverpackt, https://original-unverpackt.de/

RECUP, https://recup.de/

The Behavior Wizard, http://www.behaviorwizard.org/

Eco-indicator 99, www.pre.nl

DEEDS, www.deedsproject.org

References
Basics & Roadmap

A

1. Abrahamse, W., Steg, L., Vlek, C., & Rothengatter, T. (2005). A review of intervention studies aimed at household energy conservation. Journal of environmental psychology, 25(3), 273-291. doi: http://dx.doi.org/10.1016/j.jenvp.2005.08.002

2. Anderson, J.R. (1982). 'Acquisition of cognitive skill' Psychological Review, 89, 369–403.

B

3. Bhamra, T., Lilley, D., & Tang, T. (2015). Design for Sustainable Behavior: Using Products to Change Consumer Behavior. The Design Journal. 14:4, 427-445 Loughborough University, UK.

4. Bhamra, T., Lilley, D., Tang, T. (2008)Sustainable use: changing consumer behaviour through product design. Department of Design & Technology, Loughborough University, Loughborough, LE11 3TU

5. Bhamra, T., Lilley, D., & Tang, T. (2011). Design for Sustainable Behavior: Using Products to Change Consumer behavior, The Design Journal, 14:4, 427-445. Loughborough University, UK.

6. Brook Lyndhurst (2004). Bad Habits and Hard Choices Brook.

7. Broms, L., Bång, M., & Hjelm, S.I. (2009). Persuasive engagement: exploiting lifestyle as a driving force to promote energy-aware use patterns and behaviors. In D. Daling, C. Rust, L. Chen, P. Ashton, & K. Freidman (Eds.), Proceedings of Undisciplined! Design Research Society Conference (pp. 369/1-10). Sheffield: Sheffield Hallam University.

8. Blincoe, K., Fuad-Luke, A., Spangenberg, J.H., Thomson, M., Holmgren, D., Jaschke, K., Ainsworth, T., Tylka, K. (2009). DEEDS: a teaching and learning resource to help mainstream sustainability into everyday design teaching and professional practice. Int. J. Innov. Sustain. Dev. 4(1), 1–23.

9. Buchanan, R. (1985). Declaration by design: rhetoric, argument, and demonstration in design practice. Design Issues, 2(1) 4-22.

10. Burgbacher, G. (1991). Materialwirtschaft und Umweltschutz - Grundlagen einer schadstoffarmen Produktion. In: Burgbacher, G., and Roth, K.: Neuordnung der Abfallwirtschaft. Reihe Innovative Abfallwirtschaft. Band 1, Expert Verlag, Ehningen, pp. 35-47.

11. BUND/Misereor, (1996). Zukuftsfahiges Deutschland (Birkhauser, Basel).

C

12. Cass R. Sunstein, Nudging: A Very Short Guide, 37 J. Consumer Pol'y 583 (2014).

13. Chapman, J., Gant, N. (2007). Designers, Visionaries and Other Stories: A Collection of Sustainable Design Essays.

14. Coskun, Aykut; Erbuğ, Çiğdem (2014). User diversity in design for behavior change. Department of Industrial Design, Middle East technical University, Ankara, Turkey.

15. Crilly, N. (2011). Do users know what designers are up to? Product experience and the inference of persuasive intentions. International Journal of Design, 5(3), 1-15.

16. Crocker, R. & Lehman, S. (2013). Motivating change: Sustainable design and behavior in the built environment. Oxford, UK: Routledge.

17. Co-op Bank (2000), 'Ethical Consumerism', London, Mori.

D

18. Darnton, A. for Defra (2004). The Impact of Sustainable Development on Public behavior: Report 1 of Desk Research commissioned by COI on behalf of Defra.

19. Durning, A.T. (1992). How Much Is Enough? The Consumer Society and the Future of the Earth. W. W. Norton Company

E

20. Earth overshoot day. (2017) https://www.overshootday.org/newsroom/press-release-english-2017-calculator/ . Accessed 14.03.2018

21. Environmental Change Institute (2005). 40%house Report, Oxford University, Oxford.

22. Environmental Resources Limited (1993). Ministry of Housing, Physical Planning and the Environment: The Best of Both Worlds. Sustainability and Quality Lifestyles in the 21st Century. Publikatiereeks milieustrategie, Nr. 23. Department for Information and International Relations. The Hague.

23. Erskine, C.C. and Collins, L. (1997). Eco-labelling: success or failure? The Environmentalist 17: 125-133.

F

24. Findeli, A. (2001). Rethinking Design Education for the 21st Century: Theoretical, Methodological and Ethical Discussion. Design Issues; 19

25. Fry, T. (1993). Re-Thinking Ecodesign. Object, 43 (Autumn); 31.

26. Fogg, BJ (2017). The Behavior Wizard. Persuasive Tech Lab, Stanford University. http://www.behaviorwizard.org/wp/behavior-grid/ accessed 28/08/2017

27. Fogg, BJ (2009). A Behavior Model for Persuasive Design. Persuasive Tech Lab, Stanford University.

G

28. Galbraith, B. (2013). The Designer Nudge - Defining the Role of Design in Behavior Change.

29. Gardner, G.T. & Stern, P.C. (1996). Environmental problems and human behavior. Allyn & Bacon.

30. Gloppen, M. (2016). Nudging: How human behavior is affected by design

31. Goepel, N.; Rahme, M.R.; Svanhall, F. (2015). Strategic Recommendations for the Design of Nudges towards a Sustainable Society. Blekinge Institute of Technology Karlskrona, Sweden.

32. Government Offices of Sweden. (2016) Strategy for sustainable consumption. www.government.se/ Accessed 03.01.2018

33. Grunert, Klaus G. (2011). Sustainability in the Food Sector: A Consumer Behavior Perspective. International journal on food system Dynamics. Denmark.

34. Gust, I. (2004). Strategies to promote sustainable consumer behavior – The use of the lifestyle approach. Lund University. Sweden.

H

35. Halpern, D. et al. (2004) Personal responsibility and changing behavior: the state of knowledge and its implications for public policy Prime Minister's Strategy Unit.

36. Holdsworth, M. (2003). Green Choice, What Choice? NCC.

37. Hearne, S.A. and Aucott, M. (1991-1992). Source Reduction versus Release Reduction: Why the TRI Cannot Measure Pollution Prevention. In: Pollution Prevention Review, Winter, pp. 3-17.

38. HM Government (2005). Securing the Future: delivering UK sustainable development strategy TSO.

39. Hunnes, M.G. (2016). Annual Review of Policy Design - Original Research Nudging: How human behavior is affected by design. Norwegian University of Science and Technology. Norway.

J

40. Jackson, T. (2005). Motivating Sustainable Consumption: A Review of Evidence on Consumer behavior and behavioral Change [A Report to the Sustainable Development Research Network as part of the ESRC Sustainable Technologies Programme]. Guildford: Centre for Environmental Strategy, University of Surrey.

41. Jelsma, J. (2006). Designing 'moralized' products. In P. P. Verbeek & A. Slob (Eds.), User behavior and technology development: Shaping sustainable relations between consumers and technologies (pp.221-223). Berlin, Germany: Springer.

K

42. Kaptein, M., Lacroix, J., & Saini, P. (2010). Individual Differences in Persuadability in the Health Promotion Domain. In T. Bloug, P. Hasle, & H. Oinas-Kukkonen (Eds.), Proceedings of the 5th International Conference on Persuasive Technology (pp. 94-105) Copenhagen: Springer Berlin Heidelberg.

43. Kirman, B., Linehan, C., Lawson, S., Foster, D., & Doughty, M. (2010). There's a monster in my kitchen: using aversive feedback to motivate behavior change. In

E. Mynatt, & D. Schoner (Eds.), Proceedings of CHI '10 Extended Abstracts on Human Factors in Computing Systems (2685-2694). New York: ACM.

44. Koskijoki, M. (1997). 'My favourite things'. In Van Hinte, E. Eternally Yours: Visions on Product Endurance. Rotterdam: 010 Publishers, 132–143.

L

45.   Lilley, D. (2009). Design for sustainable behavior: strategies and perceptions. Design Studies, 30, pp.704-720.

46. Leire, C. and Thidell, Å. (2005). Product-related environmental information to guide consumer purchases – a review and analysis of research on perceptions, understanding and use among Nordic consumers. Journal of Cleaner Production 13: 1061-1070.

47. Leonard, A. (2007). The Story of Stuff.

48. Lockton, D., Harrison, D., & Stanton, N.A. (2010). The design with intent method: A design tool for influencing user behavior. Applied Ergonomics, 41(3), 382-392.

M

49. Max-Neef, M. (1989), Human scale development. New York, USA

50. Mackenzie, D. (1997). The Role and Responsibility of the Designer. Ecodesign: The Journal of the Ecological Design Association.

51. McCalley, L. T., & Midden, C. J. H. (2002). Energy conservation through product-integrated feedback: The roles of goal-setting and social orientation. Journal of Economic Psychology, 23, 589–603.

52. McDonough, W. and Braungart, M. (2009). Cradle to Cradle: Remaking the Way We Make Things. London: Vintage.

53. McKenzie-Mohr, D., L.S. Nemiroff, L. Beers, and S. Desmarais. (1995). 'Determinants of responsible environmental behavior'. Journal of Social Issues, 51: 139-156.

54. Ministry of the Environment and Natural Resources, Sweden (1993). Ecocyle Bill ready. In: Workshop Proceedings of the International Workshop on Product Oriented Environmental Policy. The Hague.

55. Ministry of Housing (1994). Physical Planning and the Environment, The Hague. Annex 6, pp. 149-151.

N

56. Narodoslawsky, M. (1993). Die Vision der Nachhaltigkeit. In: Veranstaltung-sreihe Strategien der Kreislaufwirtschaft. Tagungsband zum Symposium Forschungs- und Entwicklungsprobleme der Kreislaufwirtschaft. 23. und 24. Technische Universität Graz, pp. 37-50.

57. Narodoslawsky, M. (1992). Kreislaufwirtschaft - ein neues technologisches und ökologisches Paradigma. In: VT newsletter, 7. Jahrgang, pp. 23-26.

58. National Consumer Council. Sustainable Development Commission. (2006). I will if you will. Towards sustainable consumption. UK.

O

59. Oinas-Kukkonen, H., & Harjumaa, M. (2009). Persuasive systems design: Key issues, process model, and system features. Communications of the Association for Information Systems, 24(1), 28.

60. Overshoot Day (2017). www.overshootday.org Accessed 27.01.2018.

P

61. Paff Ogle, J., Hyllegard, K., Dunbar, B. (2004) Predicting Patronage Behaviors In A Sustainable Retail Environment. Adding Retail Characteristics and Consumer Lifestyle Orientation to the Belief-Attitude-Behavior Intention Model. Colorado State University. US.

62. Petkov, P., Köbler, F., Foth, M., & Krcmar, H. (2011). Motivating domestic energy conservation through comparative, community-based feedback in mobile and social media. In Kjeldskov, J. & Paay, J., (Eds.), Proceedings of the 5th International Conference on Communities and Technologies (pp. 21-30). New York: ACM.

63. Pratkanis, A., Breckler, S., Greenwald, A. (2014). Attitude Structure and Function. Psychology Press.

64. Pré Consultants. (2000). Eco- indicator 99 Manual for designers. Netherlands.

R

65. RAF Foundation (2012). Keeping the Nation Moving. Facts on Parking. UK.

66. Rex, E., Baumann, H. (2007). Beyond ecolabels: what green marketing can learn from conventional marketing. Journal of Cleaner Production 15: 567-576.

67. Reuters (2015). BMW's car-share service says 38 pct of clients abandon ownership. https://de.reuters.com/article/bmw-drivenow-displacement/bmws-

car-share-service-says-38-pct-of-clients-abandon-ownership-idUKL8N0Z-C3YR20150626

68. Rosenberger, G (2001). Denkanstöße zu den Zukunftsperspektiven des nachhaltigen Konsums, In U Schrader, U Hansen (Eds.) Nachhaltiger Konsum: Forschung und Praxis im Dialog (pp. 437-444). Frankfurt: Campus Verlag.

69. Roser, M., Ortiz-Ospina, E. (2018). - "World Population Growth". Published online at OurWorldInData.org. Retrieved from: 'https://ourworldindata.org/world-population-growth' [Online Resource]

S

70. Schiffman, L., Lazar L. (2015). Consumer Behavior. 11th edition. Pearson India.

71. Sinus (2015). Information 0n Sinus-Milieus®, SINUS Markt- und Sozialforschung GmbH, Heidelberg http://www.sinus-institut.de/fileadmin/user_data/sinus-institut/Downloadcenter/20150805/2015-01-15_Information_on_Sinus-Milieus_English_version.pdf.

72. Stam, F.C. (1994). Integrated Chain Management and Framework of Product Oriented Environmental Policy in the Netherlands. In: Workshop Proceedings of the International Workshop on Product Oriented Environmental Policy. The Hague, September 30th - October 1st, 1993. Ministry of Housing, Physical Planning and the Environment, The Hague, pp. 21-27.

73. Stegall, N. (2006). Designing for Sustainability: A Philosophy for Ecologically Intentional Design. Design Issues, 22(2), 56-63. doi: 10.1162/desi.2006.22.2.56.

74. Stern, P. (2000). Toward a coherent theory of environmentally significant behavior. Journal of Social Issues, 56 (3), 407-424.

75. Schäfer, M. (2002). Die täglichen Mühen der Ebene – von Ansprüchen und Widersprüchen nachhaltigen Konsumverhaltens. In G Scherhorn, C Weber (Eds.), Nachhaltiger Konsum: Auf dem Weg zur gesellschaftlichen Verankerung (pp. 63-71). München: Ökom Verlag.

76. SustainAbility. (1995). Who Needs it? Market Implications of Sustainable Lifestyles. London: SustainAbility

77. Spangenberg, J.H. (2013). Design for sustainability (DfS): Interface of Sustainable production and Consumption. SERI Germany e.V., UFZ Helmholtz Centre for Environment Research, Cologne, Halle, Germany.

78. Spangenberg, J.H. Fuad-Luke, A., Blincoe, K. (2010). Design for sustainability (DfS): the interface of sustainable production and consumption. J Clean Prod.

79. Sustainable Consumption Roundtable (2006). I will if you will - Towards sustainable consumption, May Available at www.sd-commission.org.uk/publications/downloads/I_Will_If_You_Will.pdf

80. Strategy for sustainable consumption (2016). Ministry of Finance Sweden. Sweden

T

81. Tang, T. (2010). Towards sustainable use: design behaviour intervention to reduce household environment impact.

82. Thaler, R., & Sunstein, C. (2008). Nudge: Improving decisions about health, wealth, and happiness: Yale University Press.

83. The Worldwatch Institute (2004). State Of The World. The consumer society. New York.

84. Thøgersen, J. (2002). Promoting green consumer behavior with eco-labels. In T. Dietz & P. Stern (Eds.), New tools for environmental protection: Education, information, and voluntary measures (pp. 83-104). Washington DC: National Academy Press.

85. Triandis, H.C. (1977). Interpersonal Behavior. Monterey, CA: Brooks/Cole.

86. Tromp, N., Hekkert, P., & Verbeek, P. (2011). Design for socially responsible behavior: A classification of influence based on intended user experience. Design Issues, 27(3), 3-19.

87. Trydeman Knudsen, M., Qiao Yu Hu, Luo Yan, Fonseca de Almeida, G., Santiago de Abreu, S., Halberg, N., Langer, V. (2011) Transport is important in the carbon footprint of imported organic plant products. University of Copenhagen, Aarhus University, China Agricultural University, ICROFS.

U

88. Ueda E. (2015). Aptitudes of Industrial Designers Towards Eco design - A Survey of Japanese Industrial Designers During the Early Activities of Ecodesign. Bulletin of Japanese Society for Science of Design (JSSD) 2015; 62.

89. Ueda E. (2015) Industrial Designers Working Towards and Eco-Innovation Approach. Bulletin of JSSD 2015 62 (1): 11-20.

90. UK Secretary of State for Environment, Food and Rural Affairs. (2005). The UK Government Sustainable Development Strategy. UK.

91. UN. Responsible consumption and production. Why it matters. http://www.un.org/sustainabledevelopment/wp-content/uploads/2016/08/16-00055L_Why-it-Matters_Goal-12_Consumption_2p.pdf accessed 14.03.2018

92. UN. Sustainable Development Goals. Goal 12: Ensure sustainable consumption and production patterns. https://www.un.org/sustainabledevelopment/sustainable-consumption-production/ accessed 14.03.2018

93. UNEP (2011). Decoupling natural resource use and environmental impacts from economic growth, A Report of the Working Group on Decoupling to the International Resource Panel.

94. UNEP (2016). Global Material Flows and Resource Productivity. An Assessment Study of the UNEP International Resource Panel.. Schandl, H., Fischer-Kowalski, M., West, J., Giljum, S., Dittrich, M., Eisenmenger, N., Geschke, A., Lieber, M., Wieland, H.P., Schaffartzik, A., Krausmann, F., Gierlinger, S., Hosking, K., Lenzen, M., Tanikawa, H., Miatto, A., and Fishman, T. Paris, United Nations Environment Programme.

V

95. Van Weenen H. (1999). Design for sustainable development Unknown Binding. Ireland.

96. Van Weenen, J.C. (1990). Waste Prevention: Theory and Practice. Thesis. Delft Technical University. Castricum.

97. Van Weenen, J.C. (1995). Sustainable Product Development and Waste Management. Paper presented at the 'Dublin Conference on Local Agenda 21', Dublin.

98. Veenhoven, R. (1983). The Study of Life Satisfaction. Erasmus University, Rotterdam.

99. Vermeir, I., Verbeke, W. (2006). Sustainable food consumption: Exploring the consumer "attitude–behavioral intention" gap

100. Verplanken, B. and Faes, S. (1999). 'Good intentions, bad habits and effects of forming implementation intentions on healthy eating'. European Journal of Social Psychology, 29, 591–604.

101. Verplanken, B., and Wood, W. (2006). 'Interventions to break and create consumer habits'. Journal of Public Policy and Marketing, 25, 90–103.

W

102. WCED World Commission on Environment and Development, (1987). Our common future The Brundtland report. Oxford University Press.

103.	Wood, G., & Newborough, M. (2003). Dynamic energy-consumption indicators for domestic appliances: environment, behavior and design. Energy and Buildings, 35(8), 821-841.

104.	Worldwatch Institute (2011). The State of Consumption Today. Innovations that Nourish the Planet today.

105.	Worldwatch Institute (2004). State Of The World State Of The World.

Special Focus: The Consumer Society. Washington, DC

References
Cases

Responsible consumption of plastic bags in Colombia
- http://ecoosfera.com/2010/07/la-invasion-de-las-bolsas-de-plastico-y-sus-consecuencias/
- http://www.fruitysacks.com/philosophy/
- http://www.seeturtles.org/ocean-plastic/
- http://www.theworldcounts.com/stories/interesting-facts-about-plastic-bags
- http://www.cleanup.org.au/PDF/au/cua_plastic_bag_usage_around_world_august-2015.pdf
- https://www.reusethisbag.com/reusable-bag-infographics/plastic-bag-bans-world.php
- http://www.wwf.org.co/?265410/WWF-lanza-campaa-ReemBLSAle-al-planeta
- www.soyecolombiano.com/

Thursday veggie day
- https://www.evavzw.be/fr/jeudiveggie
- Vilijoen A., Wiskerke J. Sustainable Food Planning: Evolving Theory and Practice. 2011
- https://visit.gent.be/en/thursday-veggieday?from_category=3406&context=tourist
- http://www.nycfoodpolicy.org/veggie-thursday-ghent-urban-food-policy-snapshot/
- http://www.dw.com/en/ghent-ditches-meat-and-makes-thursday-veggie-day/a-14939409

Swedish Tax breaks for repairing services
- https://archive.epa.gov/epawaste/nonhaz/municipal/web/html/
- http://ec.europa.eu/eurostat/statistics-explained/index.php/File:Municipal_waste_generated_by_country_in_2005_and_2015,_sorted_by_2015_level_(kg_per_capita).png

- https://www.mnn.com/lifestyle/responsible-living/blogs/swedish-government-wants-reward-citizens-who-repair-instead-toss
- http://www.independent.co.uk/news/world/europe/sweden-repairs-tax-waste-reduction-plan-a7318131.html
- http://www.npr.org/2016/10/02/496282845/sweden-proposes-tax-breaks-for-repairs
- https://www.pri.org/stories/2017-01-02/sweden-tries-curb-buy-and-throw-away-culture-through-tax-breaks
- https://www.theguardian.com/world/2016/sep/19/waste-not-want-not-sweden-tax-breaks-repairs

Patagonia

- http://www.wri.org/blog/2017/07/apparel-industrys-environmental-impact-6-graphics
- Claudio, L. (2007). Waste Couture: Environmental Impact of the Clothing Industry. Environmental Health Perspectives, 115(9), A449–A454.
- http://www.patagonia.com/environmental-campaigns.html
- J. B. MacKinnon (2015) Patagonia's Anti-Growth Strategy
- https://www.newyorker.com/business/currency/patagonias-anti-growth-strategy
- https://www.triplepundit.com/2011/11/patagonias-message-black-friday-dont-buy-jacket/

The Keeper menstrual cup

- National Center for Health Research, Tampon Safety. http://www.center4research.org/tampon-safety/ Accessed 27.02.2018
- Branch, F., Woodruff, T.J., Mitro, S.D., & Zota, A.R. (2015). Vaginal douching and racial/ethnic disparities in phthalates exposures among reproductive-aged women: National Health and Nutrition Examination Survey 2001–2004. Environmental Health Environ Health, 14(1)
- Ashley, R.M., Souter, N., Butler, D., Davies, J., Dunkerley, J., & Hendry, S. (1999). "Assessment of the Sustainability of Alternatives for the Disposal of Domestic Sanitary Waste." Water Science Technology 39.5 . 251-58. ScienceDirect. Elsevier Science. Web. 24 Feb. 2016.
- "Cotton vs Rayon Production Steps - Barnhardt Purified Cotton." Barnhardt Purified Cotton. Barnhardt Natural Fibers. Web. 24 Feb. 2016.
- Dodge, Matt. "Procter & Gamble to Expand Maine Tampax Factory." BDN Maine. Mainebiz, 13 Nov. 2012. Web. 12 Mar. 2016.
- Edana. Tampons From Raw Materials To Your Supermarket Shelf. Digital image. Web. 2 Mar. 2016.
- Kane, Jessica. "Here's How Much A Woman's Period Will Cost Her Over A Lifetime." The Huffington Post. TheHuffingtonPost.com, 18 May 2015. Web. 24 Feb. 2016.
- The Keeper. https://keeper.com/

Fairphone
- http://www.greenpeace.org/international/en/news/Blogs/makingwaves/smart phones-planet-toxic-waste/blog/58828/
- https://www.bcorporation.net/community/fairphone/
- https://www.fairphone.com/en/

Original Unverpackt
- https://shop.original-unverpackt.de/
- http://ec.europa.eu/eurostat/statistics-explained/index.php/Packaging_waste_statistics
- https://www.theguardian.com/sustainable-business/2014/sep/16/berlin-duo-supermarket-no-packaging-food-waste

reCUP
- http://www.dw.com/en/germanys-love-for-coffee-to-go-leaves-environmental-groups-demanding-action/a-36689719
- http://www.bbc.com/news/magazine-36882799
- www.recup.de

Freiluftsupermarkt
- Satterthwaite, D., McGranahan, G., Tacoli, C. (2010) "Urbanization and Its Implications for Food and Farming." Philosophical Transactions of the Royal Society B: Biological Sciences 365.1554: 2809–2820. PMC. Web. 30 Jan. 2018.

Partago
- Bondorová, B., Archer, G. Transport & Environment. (2017) Does sharing cars really reduce car use?
- The Guardian. What's the carbon footprint of... a new car? https://www.the-guardian.com/environment/green-living-blog/2010/sep/23/carbon-footprint-new-car. Accessed 27.02.2018
- Statista. Percentage of households owning a car in selected countries in 2014, by country https://www.statista.com/statistics/516280/share-of-households-that-own-a-passenger-vehicle-by-country/. Accessed 27.02.2018
- Partago. What we do. https://www.partago.be/wat-doen-we.html Accessed 27.02.2018

wagnisART
- Wolfe, A., Malone, E.L., Heerwagen J., Dion, J. (2014) Behavioral Change and Building Performance: Strategies for Significant, Persistent, and Measurable Institutional Change Prepared for the USA. Department of Energy under Contract
- Othman, A. (2011) Improving Building Performance through Integrating Constructability in the Design Process. British University in Egypt.
- United States Environmental Protection Agency. Sources of Greenhouse

Gas Emissions. https://www.epa.gov/ghgemissions/sources-greenhouse-gas-emissions#commercial-and-residential. Accessed 08.03.2018
- United States Environmental Protection Agency. Global Greenhouse Gas Emissions Data. https://www.epa.gov/ghgemissions/global-greenhouse-gas-emissions-data#Sector. Accessed 08.03.2018
- OECD. (2008) Household Behaviour and the Environment. Reviewing the Evidence

Icon copyright

MAKE THEM BEHAVE SUSTAINABLY

www.makethembehave.com

NOTES

www.makethembehave.com

Printed in Poland
by Amazon Fulfillment
Poland Sp. z o.o., Wrocław